T0208864

YOUR GLORIOUS, VICTORIOUS JOURNEY

Keys to Successful Christian Living

C H A R L E S   G A R R E T T

YOUR GLORIOUS, VICTORIOUS JOURNEY
KEYS TO SUCCESSFUL CHRISTIAN LIVING

Unless otherwise noted, all scripture quotations are taken from The Holy Bible, English Standard Version®, Copyright © 2001 by Crossway Bibles, a publishing ministry of Good News Publishers. Used by permission. All rights reserved.

Scripture quotations noted (KJV) are taken from the Holy Bible, King James Version.

Scripture quotations noted (NIV) are taken from the Holy Bible, New International Version®, NIV®, Copyright © 1973, 1978, 1984 by Biblica, Inc.™ Used by permission of Zondervan. All rights reserved worldwide.

iUniverse books may be ordered through booksellers or by contacting:

iUniverse
1663 Liberty Drive
Bloomington, IN 47403
www.iuniverse.com
1-800-Authors (1-800-288-4677)

Because of the dynamic nature of the Internet, any web addresses or links contained in this book may have changed since publication and may no longer be valid. The views expressed in this work are solely those of the author and do not necessarily reflect the views of the publisher, and the publisher hereby disclaims any responsibility for them.

Any people depicted in stock imagery provided by Thinkstock are models, and such images are being used for illustrative purposes only. Certain stock imagery © Thinkstock.

ISBN: 978-1-4917-7718-3 (sc)
ISBN: 978-1-4917-7719-0 (e)

Library of Congress Control Number: 2015953730

Print information available on the last page.

iUniverse rev. date: 11/17/2015

CONTENTS

FOREWORD

Anytime I am presented with a new book, I ask why. Do we need something new on this topic? Is it really "new"? Will I learn something new or gain a new perspective? Too often I am disappointed, but not this time. This book should be recommended reading for Christian leaders and students everywhere.

Charles Garrett has brought a new dynamic to successful Christian living by taking concepts that are typically reserved for business and applying them to personal spiritual success. His perspective is both fresh and well seasoned through personal experience. Upon my first review, the quotes and one-liners captured my attention to such an extent that I asked Charles where the quotations originated. He answered that they were his. After working more closely with Charles recently, I have found that he is a wealth of such succinct wisdom.

Charles is uniquely qualified to write such a book. Here is a man who understands leadership, people management, relationships, and the simple trial and error of life. He has now aptly applied this experience to excellence in life. After a full career in civil service and the National Guard, he entered higher education. I count it an honor to call Charles Garrett both colleague and friend.

—Dr. Lee Barnett, President, Legacy Christian University, Huntsville, Alabama

ACKNOWLEDGMENTS

I want to thank a few folks who contributed to this work in some way.

First, I want to thank my wife, Judy. You are my absolute best friend in the world. Your faith, encouragement, suggestions, and unwavering belief in me cannot be valued adequately. This book is dedicated to you.

Thanks to Kevin Phillips, our friend for many years, for your great suggestions and encouragement. All our dreams will become reality someday.

Thanks to Karin Dates for making me feel that this book could actually be a success, and for staying up all night reading the first draft.

Thanks to Darel Veal (a.k.a. the Librarian). I realize that asking you for a review was a great imposition with everything you have to handle in your life at this time. Your comments and suggestions were invaluable. Your crown will surely be great, not only for helping me but even more for being the wonderful friend, husband, father, and father-in-law that you are to your family.

Thanks to Mark Beaird for offering valuable advice and insight into the world of having a book published. I wish you much continued success with your own work.

Most of all, thanks to my Father, God, for creating me with a purpose; my Lord and Savior, Jesus Christ, for the ultimate gift of salvation; and the Holy Spirit, without whose guidance and insight into the Word this work would have not been possible. Thank You, Lord, for the inspiration to put this together.

Also, I am sure that there were many who offered prayers whom I do not know personally. If you are one of those people and are reading this book, thank you.

And finally, thank you, dear reader. I hope and pray that something you find in these pages will be an inspiration to you as you seek to live your own successful life as a Christian.

INTRODUCTION

Life is a journey, and a successful journey requires an accurate, up-to-date map. Sadly, many people never find their maps. Even sadder, many others strike out on their journeys and never realize they need a map, or that a map even exists.

Yet, we spend literally billions of dollars every year in endless pursuit of a sure-fire formula—a map—for success. We buy books and audio and video programs, attend seminars and workshops, sit mesmerized in front of late-night infomercials with our credit cards at the ready, and in some cases of last-resort desperation even seek advice from a psychic, all in an effort to make our journeys easier and our destination surer.

Success may be defined in myriad ways: reaching the top in one's career, accumulating a certain quantity or value of assets, marrying the perfect spouse, traveling the world, and on and on. However, success is *not* the accumulation of things, *not* an amount of money, and *not* a new house or a new BMW in the driveway. Any of these may make you *feel* successful, but only for a while. Let me say from the start that if these define success for you, then, my friend, you have missed the point. You will find that true success is not a destination but a journey.

Your journey does not begin when you reach adulthood or when you graduate from college. It does not begin when you get married or join the military or start your business or have your first child. It does not begin when you are born or even when you are conceived. Your journey begins in the mind of God, who created you for a unique purpose.

The truly successful Christian will not trouble his or her mind with "things." First of all, Christian success—our journey, if you will—involves having the mind of Christ and His attributes working in your life. Christian success involves helping others. It involves sacrifice, and it will inevitably involve periods of spiritual warfare; so in addition to a map, you also need a battle plan. Once you realize and accept this, you can begin to unlock the mysteries of your life's journey and to do that you need a key—a whole set of keys, in fact.

The keys I present here are not new. In one form or another they are the same keys you will find in any other book on success. But in addition to being worded a bit differently, the keys I offer you in this book are to be applied differently and they represent a different perspective. God tells us in Isaiah 55:8, "For my thoughts are not your thoughts, neither are your ways my ways, declares the Lord."

Part 1 presents the strategic keys. These will help you identify and clarify your purpose in life and help lay out the route by which you will arrive at your ultimate destination.

Part 2 covers the tactical keys. These are the mileposts along your journey that will ensure that you're headed in the right direction. These keys represent your master plan, your detailed road map, and they involve a more detailed level of thinking compared to the strategic keys.

Finally, in part three, we find the action keys. These are the day-to-day, step-by-step actions that are absolutely necessary to make everything else work. This is where the rubber meets the road.

If you are looking for the latest breakthrough formula, some new-and-improved shortcut for success, you will not find it here. My goal in presenting the keys to Christian success is to help you find the map for your journey through life as a Christian, and a battle plan to help you fight the attacks of the enemy. The keys are tried and true techniques that, if applied diligently, will ensure a successful Christian journey, as well as give you the tools to help someone else along the way. They may also be applied to any goal you may have in life, for the strategies, tactics, and actions presented within this book will guide you toward any destination you set out to reach. The focus, however, is on living the Christian life successfully.

My prayer for you is that these keys, along with your personal Bible study, devotional time, prayer, and fellowship with other Christians will be a great blessing along your glorious, *victorious* journey.

PART 1

STRATEGIC KEYS

Strategy—The science or art of military command as applied to the overall planning of large-scale combat operations. The plan of action resulting from the practice of this science.

Strategic—Of or pertaining to strategy. Important or essential in relation to strategy. Essential to the effective conduct of war. Designed to destroy the military potential of an enemy.

Strategist—One who is skilled in strategy.

For we do not wrestle against flesh and blood, but against the rulers, against the authorities, against the cosmic powers over this present darkness, against the spiritual forces of evil in the heavenly places.

—Ephesians 6:12

Part 1 introduces the strategic keys *discover your purpose, declare your principles,* and *determine your priorities.* These are the *why* keys. Rather than providing the detailed lines on a map that represent incremental, everyday steps toward a single objective, the strategic keys are more of a compass direction. They define the overall goal.

Strategy is not so much where you make plans; it's where you dream, where you allow God to place desires into your spirit. It's where seeds are planted that, with great care, will bloom into the fruit of great success.

What is your purpose?

A purpose is something you discover. It's already there. It's always been there. You've lived your life by it, perhaps without fully realizing it. (Although when you do discover it, you will know that you've known it all along.)

A purpose is a simple, positive statement of why you are here. It usually begins, "I am …" and is only a few words long …

A purpose is like a heart. You don't create a heart, but, like the Tin Man in *The Wizard of Oz*, you can discover the one you've always had.[1]

CHAPTER 1

DISCOVER YOUR PURPOSE

Everything in creation has a "calling" from God. We see it in such things as how the planets have been placed—the perfect placement of the sun's distance from the earth in order for life to be sustained. If the sun was closer to earth than it is, or farther than it is, most of our planet would be uninhabitable.

We see it in nature—an equilibrium, a unity, an "ecological balance" that must be maintained for life. Everything in the ecological system has an important place, a purpose to fulfill—a "calling."[2]

Everything that exists has a purpose. The account of the Creation in the first chapter of Genesis identifies the specific purposes of some of the elements of God's creation:

- In verse 6, the firmament divides the waters from the waters.
- In verse 14, lights divide day from night, for days, seasons, and years.
- In verse 15, the sun rules the day, and the moon rules the night.

Everything Has a Purpose

Everything has a reason for being, humanity included. In Genesis 1:26–28 and 2:15 we find three major purposes for which God created mankind:

1. *To have dominion over the earth*, and over every other living creature. Have you ever noticed that almost every creature on earth has an innate fear of people? This is not by accident, or some evolutionary chance, but by divine design. Humans are to have dominion over God's creation. (See also Psalm 8:3–4.)
2. *To populate the earth.* In verse 26, God establishes another of the purposes of humanity. In verse 28, God speaks directly to His creation and commands, "Be fruitful and multiply and fill the earth …"
3. *To work and care for the earth.* The principle of work is divinely inspired. Humans were not put on earth to be idle and do nothing. Even in Paradise,

God wanted people to be gainfully occupied. God showed great pride in His creation by entrusting His creation to humankind. God could have created everything so that it would need no care, but his highest creation—humans—needed something to care for. God created people and their purpose in order to sustain their lives.

We Can Know Our Purpose

While we cannot fully know the mind of God or His thoughts in creating the world, we can see that individuals have a specific purpose in God's master plan.

Let's look another passage that shows this. Psalm 139:13–15 says,

> For you have formed my inward parts; you knitted me together in my mother's womb. I praise you, for I am fearfully and wonderfully made. Wonderful are your works; my soul knows it very well. My frame was not hidden from you, when I was being made in secret, intricately woven in the depths of the earth.

This passage lets us know that God knows us even before we are born. Tracing the Hebrew words from which the phrase *you have formed my inward parts* is translated, we find the root word, *Kalah*, which means to end or complete. Now picture this: while you were still in your mother's womb, God had already completed His plan for your life.

Jeremiah 1:5 tells us, "Before I formed you in the womb I knew you, and before you were born I consecrated you; I appointed you a prophet to the nations." Have you ever known someone who said something like, "I have known ever since I was a kid what I was going be"?

In Nehemiah 2:12, Nehemiah says, "And I told no one what my God had put into my heart to do for Jerusalem." God had chosen Nehemiah to lead the effort to rebuild the walls of Jerusalem, which had been destroyed years earlier. Whether God chose Nehemiah early in his life, we do not know. We do know, however, that God's speaking to Nehemiah's heart followed a time of weeping and mourning, fasting and prayer. (See Nehemiah 1:4–11.)

Looking at Romans 12:1–2, we find Paul encouraging the members of the church in Rome to "present your bodies as a living sacrifice, holy and acceptable to God, which is your spiritual worship. Do not be conformed to this world, but be transformed by the renewal of your mind, that by testing you may discern what is the will of God, what is good and acceptable and perfect."

If I may take a bit of theological license here, let's look at God's will this way. God's will is good, period. However, I believe that sometimes He allows us to have our own way—His acceptable will. This may not be what is best for us, but He will teach us something through this experience, if we allow Him. Finally, after we have had enough of trying it our way, we will repent, and accept and strive to live in God's *perfect* will, and in discovering God's will, we will discover our own purpose.

We Have a Choice

Unlike every other creature God made, we have the power to choose. We are not driven by blind instinct; we are directed by the sum of the many small choices we make every day, good or bad, right or wrong.

Consider Moses. When God called him to lead the children of Israel out of Egypt, the first thing he did was begin to tell God why he couldn't do it (Exod. 3–4). I can't speak to the people. Nobody will listen to me. What will I say? Whine, whine, *whine*! In fact, the first word out of Moses's mouth after God called him was *but*. Exodus 4:14 tells us that God was angry with Moses. Now I don't know about you, but I don't want God angry with me. Eventually Moses conceded and, well, we know the rest of the story.

Isaiah is an example of one who seemed a bit more eager to fulfill God's calling. When the Lord said, "Whom shall I send?" Isaiah was quick to answer, "Here I am. Send me." I can almost picture Isaiah jumping up and down like a little kid on the playground, his hand high in the air as he yells, "Pick me! Pick me!"

There is one great example in the Old Testament of a man who did not—at first—obey God's call. His name was Jonah, and he ran away from his calling. Being an Israelite, he was probably afraid of the prospect of going to Nineveh, an avowed enemy of Israel. God, however, could see what Jonah could not see. Even after Nineveh repented, Jonah was angry. It seems he would have preferred to have Nineveh destroyed (one less enemy to worry about) than to have them repent. Jonah may not have known God's purpose for his life at first, but he certainly did after God called him to preach to Nineveh. He had a choice to obey God's calling, but he choose a different route instead, one that landed him squarely in the belly of the whale.

You too have a choice. You can follow God's plan and direction, or you can choose your own path and end up, as it were, stuck in a whale's digestive system.

Our Plans—God's Purpose

When we make plans for our lives, as we should, we must remember to put God first. Putting God first will help ensure that we stay "on purpose." With God as the center of our focus, our plans will ultimately succeed. Without God, even the most carefully laid and calculated plans, no matter how grand the intent, will ultimately fail.

"Many are the plans in a man's heart, but it is the Lord's purpose that prevails" (Prov. 19:21 NIV).

"In his heart a man plans his course, but the Lord determines his steps" (Prov. 16:9 NIV).

"The steps of a good man are ordered by the Lord …" (Ps. 37:23).

When God directs us, we can be sure we will not step off into some quagmire or quicksand but onto solid rock.

Sometimes when we are going along, doing what we think is right, God steps in and says, "Whoa!" This happened to Saul. He was doing his job and doing it quite well. But there was just one little detail: his job was killing Christians! Jesus stepped in and stopped Saul dead in his tracks on his way to Damascus. Jesus told Saul it was time to stop using his zeal for persecuting Him and start using it to spread the gospel, which he did with great success.

After his conversion, Saul (Paul) teamed up with Silas and Timothy. They spent some time preaching in Phrygia and Galatia, and afterward they wanted to go to Asia. But the Holy Spirit said *no*! They then tried to go to Bythinia. Again, *no*! God wanted Paul and Silas in Macedonia (Acts 16). Many of us are like that today. We want to do things our way, even though God wants to take us down another path.

In Philippi, the largest city of Macedonia, Paul and Silas encountered a woman possessed by a spirit of divination. After putting up with this for a while, Paul cast this evil spirit out of the woman. This angered the men who owned this woman because they were profiting through her fortune-telling business. (And you thought psychic readings were a new thing.) For this, the city officials had Paul and Silas thrown into prison, where later the famous "hymn singing at midnight" scene happened and they were miraculously released from prison (Acts 16:25–34).

So remember the following:

- You were created with a unique purpose only you can fulfill.
- You must discover that purpose.
- You have a choice whether to fulfill your purpose, or not.
- God will direct you if you submit to His will and allow Him.
- Our plans do not always line up with God's purpose.
- God's plans and purposes are always best for us.

CHAPTER 2

DECLARE YOUR PRINCIPLES

A principle may be defined as a law, rule, or standard, especially of good or moral behavior, as well as a predetermined or fixed policy or course of action.

Whether we consciously acknowledge them or not, we live by certain fixed laws or principles. Take the law of gravity, for example. We may ignore it, but we will surely suffer the consequences when we defy it. The principles by which we choose to live will work as surely as the law of gravity. So why not declare principles of good, truth, and righteousness as your standard of conduct?

Our principles are closely tied to our purpose; in fact, our purpose is the umbrella under which all the other keys reside. Our principles begin to define our actions and behaviors in such a way that we stay "on purpose."

Founded on Truth

In the complex process of building a bridge, one of the very first steps is to drive huge pilings down to solid rock. The purpose of these pilings is to carry the load of the bridge and its traffic down to a solid foundation that will withstand those forces. Quite often the pilings are driven to a great depth before finding solid rock.

The same holds true with our principles. They must be founded on "solid rock" if they are to withstand the forces of Satan as he tries to wear us down.

"For I will proclaim the name of the LORD; ascribe greatness to our God! The Rock, his work is perfect, for all his ways are justice. A God of faithfulness and without iniquity, just and upright is he" (Deut. 32:3–4).

Let's declare here and now that the principles we choose to live by will be founded on God's Word. Paul tells young Timothy, "all Scripture is breathed out by God and is profitable for teaching, for reproof, for correction, and for training in righteousness, that the man of God may be competent, equipped for every good work" (2 Tim. 3:16–17). This should be great comfort to us as we go about establishing and declaring the foundational principles upon which we build our Christian lives.

Truth, and the principles founded upon truth, will never change. The Word of God never changes. It is from eternity to eternity, from everlasting to everlasting.

"In the beginning was the Word, and the Word was with God, and the Word was God" (John 1:1).

Just as God himself never changes, so also His Word will never change. There is no question as to the constancy of the Word of God. It has been said, "God said it, I believe it, and that settles it." This is not entirely correct. It should read, "God said it, *and that settles it, period*!" My belief or disbelief in His Word does not alter the truth and constancy of His Word one iota.

Your Principles Will Be Tested

You might be thinking it would have been easy for the folks living in Bible days to trust God. After all, they just didn't have to go through what we have to go through today. But for a moment, consider the following:

> The ancient city of Babylon was the capital city of the nation which took Judah into captivity. It can be described as a vast square, some 55 miles around its perimeter. The city was surrounded by a huge moat of running water, and beyond this were double walls, each about ninety feet high and about twenty-five feet wide at their bases. The city was built to be impregnable.
>
> Within the city was the great Procession Way, a paved street which ran through the center of the city. This street was over seventy feet wide, and each of the huge limestone slabs with which it was paved was inscribed with a prayer to the chief Babylonian god, Marduk. Along the Procession Way was the huge Ishtar Gate, a shrine to the goddess Ishtar. The vaulted opening of the gate rose thirty-five feet above the street below, and the gate itself

was overlaid with enameled tiles forming the images of bulls and dragons, no doubt in honor of the numerous Babylonian deities.

Throughout the city were idols and images, many of solid gold. One of the shrines, honoring the god Marduk, was said to have been cast from solid gold, and weighed 4,800 pounds. At today's prices (October 2013) the cost of the gold alone would be over $88 million. All in all, in Babylon there were fifty-three temples of the great gods, fifty-five shrines to Marduk, three hundred shrines to earth deities, six hundred shrines to celestial deities, one hundred eighty altars to the goddess Ishtar, one hundred eighty altars to the gods Negral and Adad, and twelve other altars to various deities.[3]

This description of Babylon tells of the conditions into which four Hebrew youths—Daniel, Hananiah, Mishael, and Azariah—were thrust. Their homeland had been taken captive, along with almost the entire kingdom of Judah. These four were chosen because of their apparent potential to become servants in the king's court. (See Daniel 1:1–7.) Now granted, this was probably better than being on the pyramid construction crew down in the Egyptian slime pits as their ancestors had been, but it was still slavery.

Notice how Nebuchadnezzar, the king of Babylon, attempted to erase the very memory of God by changing these boys' names. The battle for principles always starts in the mind, and by changing their names, the king sought to change their minds from the one true God. By constantly hearing their new names, which contained the names of Babylonian gods, they would, or so the king hoped, begin to lose their memories of God.

After their renaming, our heroes began their education and indoctrination in the Chaldean language, and in Babylonian religion, science, mathematics, astronomy, and astrology. We have no indication that the youths resisted their education. Like Moses and Joseph before them, they probably sensed some greater purpose. Let's follow Daniel and his three companions as they go through four different tests of their faith. We can learn valuable lessons in sticking to our principles from their stories.

Eat Your Veggies

The first test of their principles came when Daniel, Hananiah, Mishael, and Azariah were allotted a daily provision of food from the royal kitchen. The deal here was that the meat was probably from animals that had been offered to Babylonian gods. The consumption of such meat was forbidden under Jewish law. Leviticus 11 gives strict laws concerning what was, and what was not, to be eaten. No doubt the royal food did not measure up.

So, in defiance of the king's order, Daniel ordered up vegetable plates and water for the next ten days, declaring that they would continue to live by Jewish dietary law (Dan. 1:8–12).

Notice that this first test concerned the most basic of human needs—food and water. If Satan can make you compromise your principles in the small things, it will be much easier for him to get you with the bigger things. On the other hand, our faith, like our muscles, becomes stronger with exercise and proper use. Satan is the master of trials and tests. He will usually start by tempting us with small things. Then, if we fail those, he will move on to bigger, more consequential temptations.

Having passed this test, our heroes were set for bigger and better things.

There Is a God in Heaven

Later, Daniel had an opportunity for great reward. King Nebuchadnezzar had a dream that troubled him, and none of his magicians, enchanters, sorcerers, or Chaldeans could interpret the dream for him. So King Neb made Daniel an offer: "But if you show the dream and its interpretation, you shall receive from me gifts and rewards and great honor" (Dan. 2:6).

Daniel answers the king with a strong declaration of principle that almost jumps off the page. He shouts, "No wise men, enchanters, magicians, or astrologers can show to the king the mystery that the king has asked. *But there is a God in heaven* who reveals mysteries ..." (Dan. 2:27; emphasis added).

What a principle to declare and stand on! When all the knowledge, learning, wisdom, and trickery of humanity fail, God is there. Daniel could easily have interpreted the dream, accepted the rewards from the king, and said, "Wow, look how God has blessed me!" But he chose to give God all the glory and honor, and in doing so, he chose to declare the principle that *all* the glory is ultimately God's.

Trial by Fire

Next follows a really big test. (As you progress toward your ultimate success, notice how your trials will increase in frequency and intensity.) It seems that Nebuchadnezzar was so impressed by Daniel's interpretation of his dream that he decided to immortalize part of that dream by creating a huge image of himself made of gold and demanding the people worship it whenever they heard music played in the kingdom. Our friends, already having successfully stood up to the king over the food deal, declared their principles again. They said they would not worship the golden image of Nebuchadnezzar, or any of his gods. When the king questioned them, they declared their trust in God.

> Shadrach, Meshach, and Abednego answered and said to the king, "O, Nebuchadnezzar, we have no need to answer you in this matter. If this be so, our God whom we serve is able to deliver us from the burning fiery furnace, and he will deliver us from your hand, O king. But if not, be it known to you, O king, that we will not serve your gods or worship the golden image that you have set up." (Dan. 3:16–18)

Shadrach, Meshach, and Abednego declared that their faith was in God Himself, not just in the fact that He could or would rescue them. They were convinced that God *could* save them from the fire, but God does not respond merely to our knowledge of His ability. What God responds to—and did in this case—is our demonstration of faith in Him.

They told the king that God could but that even if He chose not to save their lives, they would *still* serve him, and not some man-made image of some lifeless god.

We are also reminded of Abraham, as he was about to sacrifice his only son, Isaac. It wasn't until Abraham had raised the knife and was about to plunge it into Isaac that the angel intervened and stopped him. God will sometimes take us to the very limit of our faith, but if our faith is firmly grounded and based in Him, and we have declared that faith, whatever He does in response will prove our faith in Him.

Lion Lockjaw

Fast-forward a few years. Daniel is now around eighty years old and is serving under a king of a different kingdom. Nebuchadnezzar has come and gone, as has his son, Belshazzar. King Darius of the Medes now rules the kingdom. Daniel has achieved quite a high standing in the kingdom. In fact, he is one of three presidents who rule over other officials.

Because of God's favor upon Daniel's life, the satraps (governors) who reported to Daniel became jealous and sought to bring an accusation against him. Finding nothing of which to legitimately accuse Daniel, these satraps devised a plot to trap him. They used the very thing that caused him to be so blessed in the first place—his daily prayer (see Daniel, chapter 6). Daniel, however, stood strong in prayer, knowing the utter foolishness of the satraps' plot. Even when King Darius had Daniel thrown into the den of lions, the *Lion of Judah* was with him.

By boldly declaring your principles, you proclaim to the world that you stand firm on the Word of God. You can stand on that solid rock of never-changing truth and on the *Rock of Ages,* Jesus Christ. By doing so you can know that no matter what you face, *there is a God in heaven,* there is *the fourth man in the fire,* and there is *the Lion of the tribe of Judah* that will go before you.

I hope you see by the examples of Daniel and his friends how declaring and standing on your principles will help you resist Satan's temptations. Principles should never change to match your circumstances. Instead, change your response to your circumstances to match your principles.

CHAPTER 3

DETERMINE YOUR PRIORITIES

The late Dr. Stephen Covey wrote about time management in his book *First Things First*, in which he states, "The main thing is to keep the main thing the main thing."[4]

What Dr. Covey really suggests, more than time management, is priority management. Priority management is based on setting priorities using the various roles one plays in life. The main principle Covey teaches is that the things that help us grow and improve should be the things to which we assign our highest priorities, and to fail to do so is to invite trouble, and even crises, into our lives.

When we understand Covey's principles of priority management, we should then spend the most time on activities that will result in personal growth and improvement. Unfortunately, many folks view cultivating their relationship with God as a low-priority activity; they only run to God when they are in trouble or when they need something from Him. Wouldn't it be much better to spend time with God, and in His Word, *before* we come to a crisis? Wouldn't it be much better to determine that He is our *first priority*?

Just as our purpose serves as our North Star, and our principles set the boundaries and guidelines for our actions and behavior, our priorities help us set targets and tell us what tactics we need to develop to move us toward success.

The Importance of God's Word

"I have not departed from the commandment of his lips; I have treasured the words of his mouth more than my portion of food" (Job 23:12). I like the King James Version of this verse, which reads in part, "I have esteemed his words more than my necessary food."

Job is saying he placed more value on God's Word than on the food he ate to maintain his life. We all know food is vital for the continuance of our physical lives. Without food we die! But the Word of God is even more vital to our spiritual lives. Without it, our souls die, eternally.

The Word of God is also important to our spiritual well-being in that it serves to keep us from sin. David says, "I have stored up your word in my heart, that I might not sin against you" (Ps. 119:11).

It is interesting that the Hebrew word translated as "stored up" in this verse is the same word that is translated as "treasured" and "esteemed" in Job 23:12. The meaning is most nearly equivalent to what we might refer to today as "to hoard." One definition of a hoard is "a hidden supply guarded for future use."

So how does this apply to God's Word? You might equate our view of the Word as a savings account. Each time we read and study God's Word, we make a deposit into our "Word account." The more we do this, the more the account grows. When Satan comes to us and tries to throw a fiery dart at us, we can dip into our Word account, make a withdrawal, and fire it back at him. Obviously, if we have not been making regular deposits, we cannot expect to have enough of the Word hoarded up, if you will, to do us much good.

Just as we wouldn't wait until we were at the point of starvation to eat, we shouldn't wait until we are spiritually starved to enjoy God's Word. Determine today that God's Word will be a top priority. We can find many answers to many of life's questions within God's Word. Time in the Word, and time in prayer, should be automatic as we start our day. Like a good, hearty breakfast is necessary for our physical bodies, a good time of Bible study and prayer is the best way to begin our day spiritually.

Treasures on Earth versus Treasures in Heaven

The thought of hoarding the Word brings us to the topic of treasures. Jesus had a lot to say about this subject in the Sermon on the Mount.

"Do not lay up for yourselves treasures on earth, where moth and rust destroy and where thieves break in and steal, but lay up for yourselves treasures in heaven, where neither moth nor rust destroys and where thieves do not break in and steal. For where your treasure is, there your heart will be also" (Matt. 6:19–21).

This passage shows the futility of placing all our trust and hope in whatever treasures we manage to gain and store up here on earth. When our priorities are right, our treasure will be in heaven with Christ. Our thoughts will be with Him. As Isaiah 26:3 tells us, "You keep him in perfect peace whose mind is stayed on you, because he trusts in you." What a wonderful promise!

The Priorities of Life

When our top priorities are things eternal, we can truly live more stress-free lives. Our hearts will be pure toward God and not divided. Jesus says in Matthew, chapter 6, that we cannot serve God and mammon, or riches. Remember— God commanded Israel, and us by extension, to have *no* other gods before Him.

When our priorities are divided between the heavenly and the earthly, we are constantly trying to maintain a relationship with God and keep the love for our treasures on earth going strong at the same time. This presents a struggle in our hearts and spirits, and it causes instability. We must remember that God knows our needs. He told us He would supply all our needs according to His riches in glory. His bank will never fail. His source will never run dry.

We need food—that's a given. We need water—that's a given. We need clothing and shelter, both givens. But notice what Jesus told Satan when he tried to tempt Him: "But he answered, 'It is written, "Man shall not live by bread alone, but by every word that comes from the mouth of God"'" (Matt. 4:4).

In John 7:37–38, He says, "If anyone thirsts, let him come to me and drink. Whoever believes in me, as the

Scripture has said, 'Out of his heart will flow rivers of living water.'"

Look also at Matthew 6:28: "And why are you anxious about clothing?" The word *clothing* embodies not only the actual cloth a person wore but also one's station, or social standing, in the community. From this we can conclude that Jesus is not just telling us not to worry about how we will provide clothing for our families or ourselves; He is also telling us not to worry about our social status. If Jesus and the Word are our priorities, He will exalt us in His time.

Know Your Weapon

Note the two phrases "It is written" and "as the Scripture has said." How can we expect to be able to follow Jesus's example if we fail to make God's Word a top priority? Jesus used the Word not only as a weapon to defend against Satan's attacks but also as an *offensive* weapon against him.

Having served in the Air National Guard for more than twenty-two years, I received frequent training in the care and use of our primary weapon, the M16 rifle. Imagine how absurd it would be for a commander to tell his troops, "Now we're about to go into combat, so I want you to go get a weapon. It's called an M16, and I'm sure you'll figure it out once the fighting starts. Just do the best you can."

That kind of nonsense would result in needless casualties. Weapon training begins in basic training and continues throughout one's military career. Soldiers, sailors, airmen, and marines are shown the basic operation of the weapon—how to load it, aim it, fire it, disassemble it, clean it, and reassemble it so that it will function properly every time. The weapon should almost become an extension of the person wielding it so that its operation is smooth and instinctive.

The lesson here is that the Word must be the top priority for a new Christian during "basic training," if you will, and this training must continue throughout the Christian's life. We must have a thorough knowledge of its parts, how those parts fit together, how to use it, how to take care of it, how to make it a part of us so that it works every time we need it. When Satan is attacking is *not* the time to try to learn the Word. We must be ready in an instant.

Our Personal Priorities

Jesus is not saying that we should be totally unconcerned with the necessities of life, however. A prudent man or woman provides for his or her family and trusts God to supply the strength and wisdom to make that happen. Jesus is saying "Put me first and I will take care of the rest and see that your needs are provided."

"Trust in the Lord, and do good; so shall thou dwell in the land, and verily thou shall be fed. Delight thyself also in the Lord, and He shall give you the desires of thine heart" (Ps. 37:3–4 KJV).

It is a firmly and eternally established truth that we can trust God to take care of us, if and when He is our highest priority. So what are your desires? What do you want from God? Determine that God is your number one priority, and all you can even imagine can be yours.

Here is one final thought about priorities: we have to learn to balance our priorities to be successful. Yes, God's

Word and prayer should always be our top priorities, but since we are physical beings living in a physical world, we cannot ignore the priorities of taking care of our bodies and making a living to take care of our families. God provides us abilities and strength to do these things if we keep Him first.

Next, in part 2, we will examine how to put your desires, goals, and dreams into words, figure out just what it will cost you, and determine how your plan for success will start to come together. So hang on. We're just getting started.

PART 2

TACTICAL KEYS

Tactics—The technique or science of securing the objectives designated by strategy; specifically, the art of deploying and directing troops, ships, and aircraft in coefficient maneuvers against the enemy.

Tactical—Of or pertaining to tactics. Characterized by adroitness in maneuvering.

Tactician—A person skilled in the planning and execution of military tactics. A clever maneuverer.

Put on the whole armor of God, that you may be able to stand against the schemes [tactics] of the devil.

—Ephesians 6:11

Part 2 introduces the tactical keys *describe your prize, decide your price*, and *develop your plan.* These are the *what* keys. This is where you solidify your dream and "put meat on the bones." It's here that you will become clear in your heart about what the dream actually is. It is also a place of critical decisions, most importantly concerning what it will cost you to be successful. Being successful here will go a long way in determining if you will be a successful Christian or if you will muddle along in mediocrity, never fully achieving what God has planned for your life.

The more time you spend with these keys, the greater your success will be, for the tactical keys form the critical link between your strategy and your action. These keys form the lines on the map and lay out the objectives in your battle plan, upon both of which your actions will be based.

CHAPTER 4

DESCRIBE YOUR PRIZE

There are many, many things we all want God to do for us. We want to see family saved, we want to know God's will for our lives, we want to see our finances turn around for the better, we want to see our churches grow, we want to be effective witnesses for Christ. We all have wants. We all have needs. In this chapter we won't concentrate so much on our needs because the Bible tells us that God knows our needs even before we ask. Instead, we will focus on how we go about making our wants and desires crystal clear.

We cannot doubt God's power to supply our needs or grant our wants and desires, provided that what we ask is in accordance with His will for our lives. But the power to have our requests granted lies largely within us. Let me repeat that: *the power to have our requests granted lies largely within us.*

Now let me explain. I am not saying that we have the power to grant ourselves anything we want. That is New-Age thinking (which really isn't new at all; Satan used that trick on Eve in the Garden of Eden). I mean that God releases His power to provide when we show our faith in Him, when we show our belief in Him, and when we act in faith on the authority of His Word. Our belief and faith in God sets His power free to do for us all He wants to do. Our own thoughts and words determine our belief. In fact, the words we say to God, to other people, or even to ourselves play a large role in determining whether we will be successful in achieving all that God has for us … or not. We see this illustrated in the following excerpt from *Releasing the Ability of God through Prayer* by Charles Capps:

> Don't Pray the Problem—I remember being in a service one night in a certain church and a lady stood up and said, "I want you all to pray for my husband, he is getting worse. He won't go to church and I have been praying for him every day for 25 years. He just keeps getting meaner."

> The Spirit of God spoke up on the inside of me and said, "She has been holding fast to the problem all these years. If she had prayed in faith, she wouldn't have prayed all those other 24 years. She would have praised Me and thanked Me that My power was working in his behalf and her husband would have been saved many years ago. But she has bound Me from the situation by the words of her mouth."

> Jesus said, "*Whatsoever things ye desire, when ye pray, believe that ye receive them.*" She

didn't desire for her husband to get meaner. She didn't desire for him to stay at home. Why was she praying that way? She was deceived by satan [*sic*] and held in bondage by the words of her own mouth.[5]

The Power of the Spoken Word

We only have to look as far as the first chapter of Genesis to discover the power of the spoken word. In this chapter, we find nine occurrences of the phrase "And God said …" After each time He spoke, a new element of creation appeared. God literally spoke all creation into existence. He created everything from nothing. While our words are certainly not on the scale of God's creative power, in one sense the words we speak do have the power to create. We cause things to happen by what we say.

Have you ever heard someone say something like, "Well, I can't help being late. That's just the way I am"? Now look at that statement closely. *I can't help being late …* In other words, nothing I do will cause me to be early. I have no control over my life. No matter how hard I try, I just can't be anything but late. *That's just the way I am …* God placed a "late gene" into my DNA. It's not my fault. I'm hardwired to be late. Nothing I can do can change that fact.

Now, as foolish as that sounds, this is actually what a lot of people believe. Otherwise, why would they continually say, "That's just the way I am … *late!*"

But what are some of the *real* reasons people are late? Here are a few possibilities:

- They haven't made being on time or early a priority.
- They don't get up on time.
- They don't do things the night before to make things easier the next morning.
- They don't believe they *can* be early.

James 3:10 says, "From the same mouth come blessing and cursing. My brothers, these things ought not to be so." It seems from what James is telling us that we have a choice. We can choose to speak good things (blessing) or we can choose to speak evil things (cursing). When we say, "I am always late," we set up a process of bringing a curse to our life. Then we start to do things that manifest that curse through our behavior. We start doing things, we may not even be consciously aware of what actually causes us to be late.

But we can turn that around. If we start saying, "I'm always on time," we start the same process, only this time in a positive direction. We start bringing blessing to our schedule. We start getting up a little bit earlier. We start doing those things that take the last-minute stresses off us. *It is in the power of our words!*

Now, whether we are late for work, late for an appointment, or late for choir rehearsal may not be life threatening. But we can carry this thinking further and see that it can become a major deal. "I tell you, on the day of judgment people will give account of every careless word they speak, for by your words you will be justified, and by your words you will be condemned" (Matt. 12:36–37).

Knowing that our very words can bring condemnation to our lives, should we not be most careful in what we say? How often do we accept Satan's provision by our words? For example, "I'm trying to get the flu ..." Well, quit trying. Or "The devil is giving me so much trouble ..." Well, give him some back. Or even, "I guess I'll just quit ..." You guess? You *guess*? Well, I *know* who my God is and I *know* what His Word says! *And He says I can have whatever I ask for, according to His Word!*

Sorry, got a little carried away there. But do you see the point? We have to quit claiming what we don't want and start claiming all that God has for us.

Our Authority to Petition God

Jesus tells us in Matthew 7:7, "Ask, and it will be given to you; seek, and you will find; knock, and it will be opened to you." Ask. Seek. Knock. *A-S-K. Ask!* God's Word tells us that our heavenly Father knows and has provided our needs; therefore, we should never worry about what we need. Does this mean we shouldn't ask Him to supply our needs? Not at all. In fact, the Bible instructs—actually, commands—us to ask. Part of what is commonly known as the Lord's Prayer contains this sentence: "Give us this day our daily bread" (Matt. 6:11). In verse 9 of this same chapter, Jesus says, "Pray then like this," or as recorded in Luke's gospel, "When you pray, say ..." (Luke 11:2).

Now, if I remember my English grammar correctly, these three sentences are known as *imperative* sentences.

Imperative means giving a command or directive. Jesus is in fact commanding His disciples—and us, by extension—to speak words (*pray* and *say*) that in turn command the heavenly Father to release (*give*) to us our daily bread.

Of course, our Father knows what we need, but through the act of asking, we are showing our faith in Him and our faith that He will supply and provide our daily needs.

"Let us then with confidence draw near to the throne of grace, that we receive mercy and find grace to help in time of need" (Heb. 4:16).

The writer of Hebrews is telling us to go on up and "knock on the door," don't be afraid, don't fear. (The King James translation reads, "Come boldly.") God is waiting for us to ask, to seek Him, and to knock on the throne room door, come in, and tell Him what we need.

Philippians 4:6 gives us a couple of conditions for approaching God's throne with our requests: "… do not be anxious about anything, but in everything by prayer and supplication with thanksgiving let your requests be made known go God."

Prayer is the method by which we enter God's throne room. Our prayers must be accompanied by supplication (humility) and thanksgiving: humility in knowing our relationship with the Almighty God, and thanksgiving in knowing that whatever we ask, He has the power to supply and that He wants to provide for our needs just as any loving father would do.

"And this is the confidence that we have toward him, that if we ask anything according to his will he hears us. And if we know that he hears us in whatever we ask, we know that we have the requests that we have asked of him" (1 John 5:14–15).

Where do we get such confidence? Look at 1 John 3:21–22: "Beloved, if our heart does not condemn us, we have confidence before God; and whatever we ask we receive from him, *because we keep his commandments*" (emphasis added).

Our Desires Must Line Up with God's

"If you abide in me, and my words abide in you, ask whatever you wish, and it will be done for you" (John 15:7). Remember that to know God's Word is to know Jesus—not just a passing, intellectual knowledge but a deep, intimate knowledge that only grows from experience. Knowing Christ in this manner will allow His Word to *abide*, or remain, in us; but in order to achieve this level of knowledge, we must constantly and continually experience Him through His Word. We must constantly refresh our minds with His Word. When His Word abides in us, we will say things like

- "I *know* God is supplying my needs";
- "I believe my family is being saved right now"; and
- "I believe I am in the center of God's will for my life."

Along with having His Word firmly planted in our minds and hearts, we are told to ask in His name, or in other words, according to His authority.

"Whatever you ask in my name, this I will do, that the father may be glorified in the Son. If you ask me anything in my name, I will do it" (John 14:13–14).

Contracting authorities, such as state departments of transportation, have what are known as "spec books." These are legal documents and publications that contain the specifications and standards for the design and construction of highways and bridges. These books generally contain three conditions that govern contractors.

The first of these conditions is "permissive" and is denoted by the word *may*. When a contractor sees the word *may*, he or she knows that he or she has options.

The second condition is "preferred," signified by the word *should*. This still allows a contractor a bit of leeway, but the implication is that the condition followed by *should* is the condition the authority prefers and strongly encourages.

The third condition is "mandatory" and is accompanied by the word *shall* or *will*. This means there is no argument. What the book says is what the contractor is to do, or his or her payment could be negatively affected.

When Jesus says shall or will, that's it, end of argument. Is it not then inconceivable that we would not ask anything in His name? When we ask in His name, our desires have no other choice but to become reality. Satan has no power over one of Jesus's *shalls*.

So long as our desires line up with God's, we have the awesome privilege of coming to Him and making our requests known, with the full confidence and knowledge that He will give us what we ask. It is only when we ask selfishly, or to our own or someone else's harm, that God will not honor our requests.

"You desire and do not have, so you murder. You covet and cannot obtain, so you fight and quarrel. You do not have, because you do not ask. You ask and do not receive, because you ask wrongly, to spend it on your passions" (James 4:2–3).

God is not in the business of showering us with gifts just so we can have things. Our desires and our goals must be in line with His plan for our lives.

"Let the words of my mouth and the meditation of my heart be acceptable in your sight, O Lord, my rock and my redeemer" (Ps. 19:14).

"Keep your heart with all vigilance, for from it flow the springs of life. Put away from you crooked speech, and put devious talk far from you" (Prov. 4:23–24).

It is not just the words we say; it's our thoughts too that we have to guard constantly. God wants all of us, not just a part, and that includes even our thoughts. What we think about is what we will eventually become, so it just doesn't make sense to constantly be thinking negative thoughts, thoughts of illness, thoughts of defeat, or thoughts of failure. Our heavenly Father wants what is best for us and stands ready to provide it.

As author Dennis Waitley puts it,

> Expect to Win. Every winner can be identified easily because of his or her positive self-expectancy. Winners expect to win. They know that so-called 'luck' is the intersection of preparation and awareness. They look at life as a very real game but not

as a gamble. They expect to win for three key reasons:

1. *Desire*—they want to win
2. *Self-control*—they know it is they who make it happen
3. *Preparation*—they are *prepared* to win. They are ready. They have learned winning habits.

Losers generally expect such occurrences as the loss of a job, bankruptcy, a dull evening, bad service, failure, and even ill health.[6]

One final thought about the prize: you must be specific. Paul tells the believers at Philippi, "Let your requests be made known to the Lord" (Phil. 4:6). How can you make something known to someone else that you are not clear about yourself? On a number of occasions Jesus asked, "What do you want me to do for you?" Jesus asked not because He didn't know but because He wanted to be sure *they* knew exactly what they wanted. We have to know, and be able to put into words, what we want God to do for us before we ask.

While it is true that God is omniscient (that is, He knows all things), I believe He wants to know that *we* know what it is we want Him to do. What's more, if we are unclear or uncertain what we want, then we hinder God from working. So give your prize a thorough and complete description. Believe and never doubt, and the prize will be yours.

Believe

The key ingredient in ensuring that we will receive the prize we seek from the Lord is belief. This is not just an intellectual belief or wishful thinking. No, this belief is a deep, settled, without-a-doubt knowing that something is true. This is the kind of belief we need to take with us when we pray:

- Believe that all things are possible. "And Jesus said to him, 'If you can'! All things are possible for one who believes" (Mark 9:23).
- Believe you will receive what you ask for. "And whatever you ask in prayer, you will receive, if you have faith" (Matt. 21:22).
- Believe you already have what you ask for. "Therefore I tell you, whatever you ask in prayer, believe that you have received, and it will be yours" (Mark 11:24).

Don't be like the guy who was praying for a mountain to be removed. When he finished praying, he got up, walked to the window, looked at the mountain, and said, "Just like I thought. It's still there."

Disciple:

> Learner; the pupil of a teacher; the adherent of a particular outlook in philosophy or religion. The Jews in NT times considered themselves disciples of Moses (John 9:28); the Pharisees had disciples as did John

the Baptist (Mark 2:18). Like John, Jesus was not an officially recognized teacher (John 7:14), but he was popularly known as a rabbi and his associates were called disciples. The word is used both of all who responded to his message (e.g., Luke 6:17) and of those who travelled with him (e.g., Mark 6:45). Discipleship was based on Jesus' call and involved exclusive loyalty to him (Mark 8:34) which might mean literal abandonment of home, business and possessions. (Mark 10:21)[7]

Through the cross God reconciled Jew and Gentile to each other and to himself. As the lowest form of execution, it illustrated Jesus' humility, a fact which Jews found hard to understand in the Messiah. The familiar, shameful sight of victims carrying crosspieces was used to illustrate the path of discipleship.[8]

CHAPTER 5

DECIDE YOUR PRICE

Along our journey toward Christian success, we will inevitably reach two intersections—points of choice—at which we can simply say, "It's not worth it." We can *discover* our unique purpose. We can *declare* those principles that will form the foundation upon which that purpose will be founded. We can *determine* our priorities, defining what is important and what is not. We can *describe* our prize in great detail and know God's will for our lives. But then come those two critical intersections, the critical choice points. We will examine one of those intersections here. (We will look at the second in chapter 7.)

All the things we have encountered so far can be a source of tremendous excitement and energy, but when we reach the first critical choice point, much of that excitement and energy can quickly dissipate. When we reach the point of realizing what living successfully as a Christian might cost—and believe me, it will cost—we will take one of two paths: we will either decide the price is just too high and abandon our dreams, or we will accept the price, pay it, and move ahead. Someone once said it this way: *life comes down to three things; decide what you want, figure out what it costs, and then pay it.*

I submit to you that successful Christian living comes down to essentially the same three things. We must first decide that we will live according to God's purpose, acknowledge that doing so will involve a cost, and then pay the cost, knowing that the reward for doing so will result in everlasting life. On the other hand, thinking that the price of our walk with God is too high in this life and choosing to go our own way will surely result in an eternity of paying an unimaginably terrible price, that of total and eternal separation from God and the eternal damnation of our soul. God always has, and always will, demand absolute loyalty. His demands may be less obvious today than in the time when He gave the Ten Commandments to Moses, but "you shall have no other gods before Me" is just as valid today as it was then. God's desire for our loyalty has not lessened one iota.

Put God First

After four hundred years in Egypt, a land that worshipped many gods, Israel had to be reminded that there was *one* true God. God told Israel that any other god would become hostile toward Him, and He would not tolerate hostility in any form for very long. From time to time we need to be reminded that we, like the Israel of old, shall have no other gods before Him.

Part of deciding the price of our success is being settled on the fact that *all* we do must begin with the acceptance that God is supreme and sovereign. One of the first things we have to decide is that God will come first, ahead of anything else that may occupy our time, effort, energy, talents, and resources.

"If anyone comes to me and does not hate his own father and mother and wife and children and brothers and sisters, yes and even his own life, he cannot be my disciple. Whoever does not bear his own cross and come after me cannot be my disciple" (Luke 14:26–27).

Now this may seem strange, knowing that God is *love*; yet here Jesus is telling us that we must hate our family, even our own lives. What is He really saying?

The Greek word translated to read "hate" in the passage is *miseo,* which actually means "to love less than …" This is different from the word translated to mean "hatred" in Galatians 5:20, describing the "works of the flesh." There the word is *echthra*, which more closely describes an enemy or a foe, as were the gods that God told us not to put before Him.

This lets us know that we can love our families, and our own lives, and still be totally and perfectly committed to God and His plan for us. He is not telling us to turn our backs on those we love and for whom we are responsible. He is only reminding us of their proper place in our overall relationship with Him.

Another aspect of putting God first is our willingness to forsake, or literally say good-bye to, our worldly possessions. God will always test our willingness to give up our goods before actually demanding that we do so. Recall Abraham and Isaac. God only required Abraham to display a willingness to sacrifice his only son, but God took him to the very edge of his commitment. The angel of God stopped him just short of the actual sacrifice. Often our willingness is the only price we need to pay. At other times it takes a full and complete sacrifice of what we possess.

Follow Christ

"Then Jesus told his disciples, 'If anyone would come after me, let him deny himself and take up his cross and follow me'" (Matt. 16:24).

What does it mean to deny oneself? Does it imply denying that we exist, denying our worthiness to follow Christ, denying our bodies the nutrition needed to live? This passage can be translated to mean, "If anyone is desiring to come after me, let him forget self and lose sight of his own interests …"

To deny self is to subordinate our goals, plans, desires, and dreams to God's plans. But here is the thing about that: when we are truly in line with God's plan, and when we allow Him to place the desires within us, it is a pleasure to deny self. In fact, when we are living successfully as Christians, we would have it no other way. We look forward to finding out what God has for us to do next. We take great pains to be sure our goals line up with His plans for us.

Count the Cost

"For which of you, desiring to build a tower, does not first sit down and count the cost, whether he has enough to complete it" (Luke 14:28)?

Your life can be compared to building a structure. Everything you do has a price. If you want to live healthy, there is a cost. Exercise costs. Education costs. Being lazy and uneducated costs. It is up to you to decide which cost is higher, and which you are willing to pay.

The church where my wife and I are members entered into a building program a few years ago. As we began to implement the program, suppose our pastor had said, "Let's build a new building. I don't know what it will cost, or how much we have available to spend, but we'll get started and just figure it out as we go." How far do you suppose we would have progressed with the building? Now, I understand there are always contingencies, things that unexpectedly come up, but you have to have a pretty good idea before ever breaking ground as to the ultimate cost of any project of that scope.

We did in fact end up with a very nice new building because the pastor and the building committee looked very carefully at the needs and resources of the church, the capacity for future growth, and where we wanted to be in a few years. They sat down together with the builder and decided the price *before* the first shovel of dirt was ever turned. Now that's counting the cost!

Take Up Your Cross

Even though our Christian walk will cost us something, our price could never compare with what Jesus paid for our salvation. While it is true that most of us will never be required to pay anything compared to the price He paid, we need to decide, as Jesus did, that whatever God requires of us, we would willingly do. Consider Jesus's price:

> The purple cloak is ripped away, but the crown of thorns remains. The death squad places a plank of unfinished wood on Jesus' shoulders. It weighs between fifty and seventy-five pounds, it is just a little less than six feet long, and its splinters quickly find their way into the open wounds of the Nazarene's body. The humiliation at Pilate's palace now complete, the procession toward the place of execution begins.[9]

The second part of Matthew 16:24 tells us to take up our crosses. This goes far beyond simply wearing a gold cross around our necks. While none of us will likely ever endure what Jesus did in taking up His cross, our price will always involve the taking up of our own personal "crosses." Jesus is prophetically speaking of His own death and in part telling His disciples that in the course of following Him, they each might reach a point of having to choose life or His plan. This would likely mean their deaths.

Again, we all have a price to pay as Christians. Ours may be as simple as sacrificing a bit of time each day to spend in God's Word, or as complete as sacrificing our life on a foreign mission field. We may never have to face such a decision. But every day we face choices that could mean life or death spiritually. Do we stand for Christ, or do we go along with the crowd? Do we risk ridicule, or do we boldly show the world that we are Christians?

Recall the shooting at Columbine High School in Colorado in 1999. One of the shooters, reportedly while pointing a gun at Cassie Bernall's head, asked her, "Do you believe in God?" How would you answer that question if asked of you under similar circumstances? How would I answer? I do not know, for I have never faced a similar test. But living successfully as Christians just might someday cause us to face questions such as this.

The Spiritual Cost

"I appeal to you therefore, brothers, by the mercies of God, to present your bodies as a living sacrifice, holy and acceptable to God, which is your spiritual worship" (Rom. 12:1). The *therefore* in this verse refers to Romans 11:36, the last verse of the preceding chapter: "For from him and through him and to him are all things. To him be glory forever. Amen."

God made our bodies, and we exist for His glory. We exist to serve Him and His purposes and nothing else. Kenneth Wuest's masterful translation of the New Testament from its original Greek suggests that the phrase *present your bodies* means "to place your bodies at the disposal of God."[10] It's not enough just to give of our resources. God wants *us*, living sacrifices. He wants our service, not just a few dollars we might give from time to time. It would be easy just to sit at home and send our check each week, or once a month, or whatever, and think we are doing our part. But if we take time to read the rest of Romans, chapter 12, and the rest of the epistle, we will discover just what Paul had in mind as reasonable:

- Don't overrate yourself.
- Use the gifts given to you.
- Love unconditionally.
- Be kind.
- Rejoice in hope.
- Take care of the needy.
- Bless your persecutors.
- Rejoice/weep with others.
- Repay evil with good.
- Don't seek vengeance.
- Obey the law.
- Pay your taxes.
- Owe no one.
- Walk decently.

This is just a partial list of the price of being a living sacrifice. These all require action beyond what is merely comfortable and easy. These sometimes involve sacrifice, especially in the area of not seeking vengeance for a wrong done to us. But, here again, if our desires line up with God's, it is a price we will gladly pay.

"Do not be conformed to this world, but be transformed by the renewal of your mind, that by testing you may discern what is the will of God, what is good and acceptable and perfect" (Rom. 12:2).

The Intellectual Cost

Besides a physical price, there is also a mental price. *Conformed* means "to be pressed into a pattern or mold." Our standard is not the world's standard, but God's. *Transformed*, on the other hand, is complete metamorphosis. Like the caterpillar that turns into a butterfly, so we are to change. How does this transformation take place?

The renewal of our minds is not a one-time-only event. A careful study of the Greek words indicates this renewal is to be a repetitious, ongoing process. In other words, it is continual. We never learn it all. We can read a verse of Scripture a hundred times and then on the hundred-and-first time find something new and fresh and applicable to a current situation in our lives. We regularly and consistently need to expose our minds to God's Word. We can do this, of course, by reading the Bible, reading good books, listening to good music, hearing messages from anointed, Spirit-filled ministers and teachers, and associating with like-minded Christians.

When we are physically, mentally, and spiritually aligned with God, it naturally follows that our resources will be aligned with His purposes as well. The story of the "rich young ruler" (Matt. 19; Luke 18) teaches us that we are either 100 percent for God or not for God at all. God doesn't want 99 percent; He wants *all* of us. There is an apparent paradox here. Like the young man in the story, if we cling tenaciously to our possessions, we will end up losing everything. If, however, we are willing to give up all we have—money, possessions, time, talent, abilities—then we will gain immeasurably more in the long run.

"Truly, I say to you, there is no one who has left house or wife or brothers or parents or children, for the sake of the kingdom of God, who will not receive many times more in this time, and in the age to come eternal life" (Luke 18:29–30).

The price for successful Christian living may seem very high, but look at the rewards. Then consider the cost of not paying the price, of not giving all to God, and the horrible consequences of that choice.

"For what will it profit a man if he gains the whole world and forfeits his soul? Or what shall a man give in return for his soul" (Matt.16:26)?

Stay in the Word

We have already explored the importance of God's Word. The Word is no less important in deciding your price than in any of the other keys we have learned about so far. We can sum it up by deciding that part of our price is staying in the Word. God's Word will ultimately tell us everything we need to know. It will define our price and at the same time give us the grace to pay it.

> Teach me, O Lord, the way of your statutes; and I will keep it to the end. Give me understanding, that I may keep your law and observe it with my whole heart. Lead me in the path of your commandments, for I delight in it. Incline my heart to your testimonies, and not to selfish gain!

Turn my eyes from looking at worthless things; and give me life in your ways. Confirm to your servant your promise, that you may be feared. Turn away the reproach that I dread, for your rules are good. Behold, I long for your precepts; in your righteousness give me life! (Ps. 119:33–40)

Psalm 119 talks about God's Word, His statutes, His precepts, His laws, His commandments, and His judgments. Our desire should be that of the psalm's writer—to intimately know about all of these. They will establish us, strengthen us, cleanse us, and keep us.

The Word is self-teaching. The more of the Word we digest, the more we desire. We need not go looking for some new philosophy, religion, or pathway to God. The Word is all we need. We must stay there. We must continue there.

"So Jesus said to the Jews who had believed in him, 'If you abide in my word, you are truly my disciples, and you will know the truth, and the truth will set you free'" (John 8:31–32).

What a promise! And what a small price to pay for the freedom that only God's truth can grant.

YOU NEED A BLUEPRINT
FOR SUCCESS

Imagine that you are an internationally known architect and that you have just received a contract to supervise the construction of the world's tallest and most beautiful building.

Your first task would be to estimate the quantity and quality of the materials required for the fabulous structure.

Then, your next step would be to ask the contractors to hire the skilled craftsmen— the steel workers, the carpenters, the brick layers, and plumbers and electricians and the common laborers required to complete the gigantic undertaking.

Now, let's suppose that you are at the building site. The building materials are piled high, the contractors are surrounded by their workmen. You give the command, "Build me a building!" The first question on the lips of every craftsman and the contractors for whom they work would be, "Where is the blueprint?"

If each of these men began to work on this great building using his own individual thought, the building would live in history as a monstrosity.

There would be no organized effort toward one common objective because the craftsmen would be 'going off in all directions at the same time.' The most likely thing to happen would be that the building would never be completed. Confusion and frustration would reign.

Your own life is a direct parallel to the building that we have been describing. You are the architect. You can construct happiness and success or a life filled with misery and failure. The blueprint is the key to the results. You must have a plan if you are going to succeed! Without a blueprint to guide your efforts, you end up confused, disillusioned and totally frustrated.[11]

You need a life map to the end of your life simply because that is the intelligent thing to do. The good and the bad will come along, but you move the bias toward the good when you have planned and mapped out your future. If you still have some doubt about planning your life, remember that God takes it even further—into eternity.[12]

CHAPTER 6

DEVELOP YOUR PLAN

I have heard it said that most people spend much more time planning their next vacations than they ever do planning the course of their lives. When it comes to higher education, the most popular major among freshmen and sophomores is "undecided." Most people end up in a career—or more appropriately, a rut—not as the result of careful planning, but by chance. This is a sad fact of life.

Putting Your Life Together

How many Christians do you know who spend any time at all planning their lives? Shouldn't we take the time to map out our lives according to God's patterns and directions, or do you think it is okay just to let life happen and hope for the best? Or as some put it, let God lead us where He wants us to go.

While it is true that God will lead us, we have a responsibility as well. We must put some thought into how we are going to live our lives if we want to live successfully as Christians. The old adage, "If you fail to plan, then you plan to fail," is as true for Christians as it is for anyone else; it's just that the consequences of failure in this respect are tragic indeed.

Why do people, especially Christians, have so much trouble planning their lives? Some answers, excuses actually, may go something like this:

- God will show me what to do.
- I don't know how to get through today, much less how to plan my life.
- If I try to plan my own life, I might do something within myself.
- God says, "Take no thought for tomorrow."

If we use these as excuses not to plan our lives, then we miss the point. In fact, I think we miss the whole concept. Let's look at how to develop your plan from God's perspective.

God's Plan—The Pattern

First of all, let's agree that God has never and will never do anything without a reason and a purpose. From the very first act of creation, God had a design and a pattern—a plan—to guide Him. He laid out the universe according to a very strict set of laws that will not be violated. Everything had a place and a function.

"And let them make me a sanctuary, that I may dwell in their midst. Exactly as I show you concerning the pattern of the tabernacle, and of all its furniture, so you shall make it" (Exod. 25:8–9).

God desired to dwell among His people, but the place for His dwelling had to fit a very precise pattern. The word *pattern* implies a structure, one in which every part has a place and fits together with other pieces to form a whole.

Exodus 26:1–6 (KJV) describes how when the tabernacle was assembled it was to become a single unit. Note how often the word *one* appears:

- Every *one* of the curtains shall have *one* measure
- Shall be coupled together *one* to another
- Take care of *one* another
- And it shall be *one* tabernacle

Without a carefully designed plan, all these parts would not have formed a unified structure. Keep this in mind, as we will come back to it later.

The tabernacle was to be a mobile dwelling place. In other words, it was not a permanent structure. When David was king, the Lord gave him the plans for a permanent dwelling place—the Temple.

> Be careful now, for the Lord has chosen you to build a house for the sanctuary; be strong and do it. All this he made clear to me in writing from the hand of the Lord, all the work to be done according to the plan. Then David said to Solomon his son, "Be strong and courageous and do it. Do not be afraid and do not be dismayed, for the Lord God, even my God is with you. He will not

> leave you or forsake you, until all the work
> for the service of the house of the LORD is
> finished." (1 Chron. 28:10, 19–20)

Notice that David did not say to Solomon, "Okay, son, I want you to build God a house. Make it, oh, about a hundred cubits or so … I don't know. Use your imagination." *No!* He passed on to Solomon the exact plan God had given to him, a written plan. (Let me interject here that if your goals and plans are not written down, they are just wishes.)

Now let's fast-forward about four hundred and fifty years. Babylon has taken Jerusalem captive, destroyed the walls of the city, and laid to waste the temple that Solomon had spent some ten years building. God, speaking through His prophet Ezekiel, has a most unusual but encouraging message: "As for you, son of man, describe to the house of Israel the temple, that they may be ashamed of their iniquities; and they shall measure the plan" (Ezek. 43:10).

So what is God saying?

First, "Describe to the house of Israel the temple," or as the King James translation renders it, "Show the house to the house." Remind my people that My plan, My pattern, is still real, still valid, and still alive.

Second, God's plans and patterns should be remembered. We need to remind ourselves (through God's Word) from time to time that He has a plan for us, and we need to be diligent in learning that plan.

Third, God's plan will point out our errors, mistakes, sins, and shortcomings. His plan will let us know when we are off course and when we need to make corrections.

Fourth, God's plan is our standard. When He says, "and they shall measure the plan," I believe He is telling us to stretch ourselves to measure up to His plan, not our own so much. We must stretch and conform to His plan, but that is the only way we can grow and become successful as Christians.

"For as in one body we have many members, and the members do not all have the same function, so we, though many, are one body in Christ, and individually members one of another" (Rom. 12:4–5).

Remember how the plan for the tabernacle described every part as fitting together so that it became one tabernacle? There were many, many individual parts, but when they all worked together, each in its place, the plan worked and the tabernacle became a very strong unit, built for and functioning according to God's purpose.

The Plan for the Individual

So it is with us today. As God's dwelling place, the Temple of the Holy Spirit, we are made up of many members, many gifts, many skills, many abilities, and many talents. It is up to us to discover our unique purpose, how all these things fit together within that purpose, according to God's plan and pattern for our lives, and then develop our plan for using what He has given us.

> Having gifts that differ according to the grace given to us, let us use them; if prophecy, then in proportion to our faith; if service, in our serving; the one who teaches,

in his teaching; the one who exhorts, in
his exhortation; the one who contributes,
in generosity; the one who leads, with
zeal; the one who does acts of mercy, with
cheerfulness." (Rom. 12:6–8)

This is why discovering your purpose is so critical. It shows you where to concentrate your effort to maximize your effectiveness. If, for instance, your purpose is to be an encourager (exhortation), then your plan might develop like this:

- Pray that God will put me in touch with people who need encouragement.
- Read and study books on encouragement.
- Learn, practice, and develop listening skills to that I can pick up subtle keys from people who might not realize or openly admit that they are discouraged.
- Make an effort to find out special dates such as people's birthdays, anniversaries, etc., and send a special card or small gift.
- *Encourage myself* (Josh. 1:9).

Once you realize and accept the following truths, then you will be on your way not only to discovering your purpose but to fulfilling it as well:

1. God has always had a plan and a pattern for you.
2. God sanctions planning on your part.
3. You are part of a greater plan.

4. You fit together with others when you don't try to be something you cannot or are not supposed to be.

5. Your part and your plan are just as important to God and His plan as anyone else's.

Throughout the Bible, you can find many "plans" for life: the Ten Commandments, the Sermon on the Mount, and the Epistles, to name a few. One simple set of guidelines is 1 Thessalonians 5:16–23. I mention this passage for a few reasons:

1. The instructions are simple and easy to understand.

2. There are seven directives—the Biblical number of perfection or completeness.

3. They don't require special skill or knowledge to practice.

So let's take a look.

1. *Rejoice always* (1 Thess. 5:16). To be successful, any endeavor must begin with an attitude of joyfulness. Knowing how successful the plans God used throughout the Old Testament were, we should always rejoice in our plans, provided they match with God's. Taking the meaning of the word *rejoice* to its fullest extent, we are to pass our rejoicing, or actually our cheerfulness, on to others.

2. *Pray without ceasing* (1 Thess. 5:17). This should go without saying, but Paul obviously thought it necessary to mention. When our plan is developed, we should pray that God will bring it to full maturity. Paul is not saying that we should pray

continuously, without stopping to do anything else. That would not only be impractical but also be impossible. He is saying we should pray *until that for which we are praying has come to pass*, and continually maintain an attitude of prayerfulness and thanksgiving to God.

3. *Give thanks in all circumstances* (1 Thess. 5:18). Just as Paul tells us to rejoice, our planning should be grounded in an attitude of thankfulness and gratitude. Even in a dire trial, we can have an attitude of thankfulness. Romans 8:28 teaches us, "for those who love God, all things work together," and Psalm 46:1 says, "God is our refuge and strength, a very present help in trouble." If all we had were these two passages, then we would know enough to be eternally thankful.

4. *Do not quench the Spirit* (1 Thess. 5:19). Quench, in this sense, is to hold down, to suppress or extinguish. The Holy Spirit will do wonderful things for us, but only to the extent we allow Him. He will not force Himself upon anyone. What's more, we have the choice to allow Him to work in us, but choosing not to can prevent Him from working fully, if we quench the Spirit.

5. *Do not despise prophecies* (1 Thess. 5:20). This verse ties into and fits with the next.

6. *But test everything. Hold fast to what is good* (1 Thess. 5:21). Prophesying covers a broad spectrum of activities from preaching, to speaking a message from the Holy Ghost, to divinely knowing something about another person, to literally telling things that

will happen in the future. We are told in verse 20 not to automatically dismiss a prophecy as bad. However, following in verse 21, we are cautioned to screen everything we hear as prophecy through the Word and with the leading of the Spirit, and retain only that which fits the pattern. By implication, we are to discard anything that does not measure up. The only way we are able to do this is to intimately know the *real*. How we do that? As we have already seen, we come to know God and His truth only through continually investing time in His Word and prayer. Any plan we undertake simply must include these activities.

7. *Abstain from every form of evil* (1 Thess. 5:22). We are to avoid anything that would be harmful to us, to the Body of Christ, or to God's plan for our lives. We have to carefully guard our senses and be sure that only good things enter our souls and spirits.

Just as the Temple of Solomon became corrupted when the people forgot the laws of God and deviated from the pattern, so can we if we fail to follow the plan and fit the pattern that God has developed for us. Be diligent in knowing God's plan, and be diligent in developing *your* plan. Like David and Solomon, we can be assured that God will never fail us. He will never forsake us. He will see our plans through to completion. All we have to do is be sure our plans line up with God's plans and that we fit His pattern. Then we will be successful as Christians.

ACTION KEYS

Action—the accomplishment of a goal or task, usually over a period of time, in stages, or with the possibility of repetition; the most vigorous, productive, or exciting activity in a particular field or area.

> "Whatever your hand finds to do,
> do it with your might …"
> —Ecclesiastes 9:10a

Part 3 introduces the action keys *deploy your parachute, discuss your progress,* and *deliver your proof.* These are the *how* keys. It is here that the rubber meets the road, where all your strategizing and planning is put to the test. It is also here that all the work you have done before can languish on the shelf and never bring the success you were meant to achieve, *if* you do not put that work into *action.*

The Bible teaches us that to know to do good and not do it is sin. God took time to carve your unique fingerprints and to make you different from every other living creature on earth. You should do nothing less to honor and praise Him than everything you can to become a successful Christian. Remember that it's not all up to you; God will meet you more than halfway. You take one step, He will take a million, but only when you take that first one.

So don't hesitate. Get going. You have a lot of life left, so make it count.

Be that successful Christian God wants you to be.

The Scroll Marked IX

My dreams are worthless, my plans are dust, my goals are impossible.

All are of no value unless they are followed by action. *I will act now.*

Never has there been a map, however carefully executed to detail and scale, which carried its owner over even one inch of ground. Never has there been a parchment of law, however fair, which prevented one crime. Never has there been a scroll, even such as the one I hold, which earned so much as a penny or produced a single work of acclamation. *Action*, alone, is the tinder which ignites the map, the parchment, this scroll, my dreams, my plans, my goal, into a living force. Action is the food and drink which will nourish my success. *I will act now.*

My procrastination which has held me back was born of fear and now I recognize the secret mined from the depth of all courageous hearts. Now I know that to conquer fear I must always act without hesitation and the flutters in my heart will vanish. Now I know that action reduces the lion of terror to an ant of equanimity. *I will act now.*

I will not avoid the tasks of today and charge them to tomorrow for I know that tomorrow never comes. Let me *act now* even though my actions may not bring happiness or success for it is better to act and fail than not to act and flounder. Happiness, in truth, may not be the fruit plucked by my action yet without action all fruit will die on the vine. *I will act now.*

I will act now. For now is all I have. Tomorrow is the day reserved for the labor of the lazy. I am not lazy. Tomorrow is the day when the evil become good. I am not evil. Tomorrow is the day when the weak become strong. I am not weak. Tomorrow is the day when failure will succeed. I am not a failure. *I WILL ACT NOW.*"[13] (emphasis added)

Fear or Faith?

Fear can be broken down into three levels. The first level is the surface story ... This level of fear can be divided into two types: those that 'happen' and those that require action.

One of the insidious qualities of fear is that it tends to permeate many areas of our lives. For example, if you fear making new friends, it then stands to reason you also may fear going to parties, having intimate relationships, applying for jobs, and so on.

This is made clearer by a look at the second layer of fear, which has a very different feel from Level 1. Level 2 fears are not situation-oriented; they involve the ego.

Level 2 fears have to do with *inner states of mind* rather than exterior situations. They reflect your sense of self and your ability to handle this world. This explains why generalized fear takes place. If you are afraid of being rejected, this fear will affect almost every area of your life—friends, intimate relationships, job interviews, and so on. Rejection is rejection—wherever it is found. So you begin to protect yourself, and, as a result, greatly limit yourself. You begin to shut down and close out the world around you.

Level 3 gets down to the nitty-gritty of the issue: the biggest fear of all—the one that really keeps you stuck. Are you ready?

LEVEL 3 FEAR
I CAN'T HANDLE IT!
AT THE BOTTOM OF EVERY
ONE OF YOUR FEARS
IS SIMPLY THE FEAR THAT YOU CAN'T HANDLE
WHATEVER LIFE MAY BRING YOU.

The truth is:

IF YOU KNEW YOU COULD HANDLE ANYTHING
THAT CAME YOUR WAY,
WHAT WOULD YOU POSSIBLY HAVE TO FEAR?
The answer is: NOTHING!"[14]

CHAPTER 7

DEPLOY YOUR PARACHUTE

I have often asked the question, why would anyone want to jump out of a perfectly good airplane? A bit tongue-in-cheek, I'll admit, but it does serve to introduce this chapter. Deploying one's parachute simply says that there comes a time when it is time to act, to do something. The best laid plans of mice and men … well, are just that, laid-up plans if the planner never acts upon them.

Recall that in chapter 5, "Decide Your Price," we talked about two critical choice points everyone will encounter along his or her journey to Christian success. At the point when you begin to decide what your price will be, you can say, "It's not worth it" or "The price is just too high." Hopefully, you will say, "Yes, I'll pay whatever price I have to pay in this life, knowing the reward in my eternal life to come will far outweigh anything here."

Now we come to the second critical decision point. Sadly, this is where most Christians fail. In fact, this is the point at which most people fail in any goal-setting plan.

At this point it simply comes down to "Am I willing to do whatever it takes to succeed?"

What causes people to fail? What stops people with talent, ability, and apparently all the necessary equipment from pushing through the barriers and going on to success? What prevents us from fully experiencing all that God has for us? What is the one thing that keeps us from doing what we know we should do? I believe it is *fear*.

The Fear-Faith Continuum

Fear   Faith

←--→

Paralysis   Action

Look carefully at the illustration of what I call the fear-faith continuum. Notice how fear and paralysis are close companions. Now I'm not talking about physical paralysis caused by disease or an accident. No, this paralysis is caused by your fears; fear will immobilize you and make it seem impossible for you to move.

On the opposite side of the continuum is faith and action. Just as faith will overcome fear, so will action overcome paralysis. Do something, do anything, but get off square one!

There Is No Reason to Fear

Where does fear come from? The simplistic answer is, of course, from Satan.

"For God gave us a spirit not of fear but of power and love and self-control" (1 Tim. 1:7). The literal translation from the Greek word for fear is "timidity." When we are timid, we tend to hesitate. We tend not to act when opportunity comes our way, but we have no reason to be timid, ashamed, or fearful. As Christians, our lives should roar like a lion, for the Lion of Judah resides within us.

"The Lord is my light and my salvation; whom shall I fear? The Lord is the stronghold of my life; of whom shall I be afraid" (Ps. 27:1)?

When you were a child—or maybe even now as an adult—and you were afraid of the dark, what is the one thing that would help ease your fears? Light, of course! Light chases the monsters from under the bed. Light exposes objects that are making those eerie shadows on the wall. When something makes us afraid, for whatever reason, all we have to do is remember *whos*e children we are. Our Father will come into our room and shine His great light all around us, exposing all the hidden things Satan is trying to throw at us. God's glorious light will chase away the evil and the terror. As Psalm 23:4 says, "I will fear no evil, for you are with me."

But When We Do …

David knew plenty of times when he was afraid, but he also knew who his Great Shepherd was. He knew God was protecting him as only one who cares for sheep can do. Certainly there is no situation, no person, and no thing we should be afraid of. But in times when we are afraid, it should be a great comfort to us to know that even if fear overwhelms us, God is there to help. There is great comfort in knowing God is always there to help us when we fear. David, the mighty king, personally knew times of fear.

> God is our refuge and strength, a very present help in trouble. Therefore we will not fear though the earth gives way, though the mountains be moved into the heart of the sea, though its waters roar and foam, though the mountains tremble at its swelling. (Ps. 46:1–3)

In Alabama, my home state, we're right in the middle of "Tornado Alley," and tornados can be extremely destructive and frightening. If you live in Southern California, you might fear earthquakes. In Hawaii, volcanoes might constantly be on your mind. For those living along the Pacific Rim, the threat might be tsunamis. For the Gulf Coast and the Caribbean, it's hurricanes. And nowadays, it seems we are gearing up for a long overdue asteroid strike. The point is that you can always find something to cause worry and fear if you look long enough.

But remember that God is our refuge. The Hebrew word for refuge is *machaceh* and means a place of shelter and protection from storms. Another meaning of the word suggests protection from falsehood, as in Satan's attacks. Remember that Satan is the father of lies. This lets me know

- when tornados threaten, *God has His way in the whirlwind;*
- when earthquakes shake our world, *God is our solid rock;*

- when volcanoes heat up, *He is the fourth man in the fire;*
- when tidal waves threaten like a flood, *the Spirit lifts up a banner against the enemy;* and
- when Satan hurls "asteroids" at us, *we can run to God for protection.*

"When I am afraid, I put my trust in you" (Ps. 56:3). How wonderful it is to know that even though we have no reason to fear, when fear does overcome us, we have a source of strength and peace that *no* fear can overcome!

Action Dispels Fear

So how do you break the grip of fear? How do you move from paralysis to action? *You act, that's how!* Okay, I know what you're thinking. That sounds too easy, too simple. But it really is true. To break out of the fear that keeps you from doing what you want to do, you have to *do what you want to do,* or more precisely, what God wants you to do.

"But someone will say, 'You have faith and I have works.' Show me your faith apart from your works, and I will show you my faith by my works" (James 2:18).

"For as the body apart from the spirit is dead, so also faith apart from works is dead" (James 2:26).

It is one thing to have great faith, but remember this: *when it's all said and done, more gets said than done.*

The NIV translates James 2:18 this way: "Show me your faith without deeds, and I will show you my faith by what I do." In other words, faith is not something you have. *No no no!* Faith is something you *do!* Where there is fear, there are no works (that is, no *action*). Where there is action, it follows that there must be faith, which is demonstrated by that action.

To further prove that fear prevents us from acting, look at the Parable of the Talents:

> He also who had received the one talent came forward, saying, "Master, I knew you to be a hard man, reaping where you did not sow, and gathering where you scattered no seed, *so I was afraid*, and I went and hid your talent in the ground. Here you have what is yours." (Matt. 25:24–25; emphasis added)

This servant's fear cost him dearly. The others were well rewarded for their efforts, but not this one. By not taking any action, he lost not only what he had, but also all he could have had.

Wuest says it like this: "Moreover, keep on becoming doers of the Word and stop being hears only, reasoning yourselves into a false premise and thus deceiving yourselves …"[15]

Think of it this way: there is anecdotal, if not empirical, evidence that suggests a person will retain only 5 percent of what he or she hears, 10 percent of what he or she sees, but 85 percent of what he or she does.

So if we only hear the Word when we are at church on Sunday morning, and we let our fear keep us from putting what we have heard into action, we can only expect a 5 to 10 percent success rate at best. On the other hand, when you *deploy your parachute*—that is, when you commit to God's service and put your commitment into action—you can expect much greater success than you ever thought possible.

"Whatever your hand finds to do, do it with your might …" (Eccles. 9:10a).

"Whatever you do, work heartily, as for the Lord and not for men …" (Col. 3:23).

"And you shall love the Lord your God with all your heart and with all your soul and with all your mind and with all your strength" (Mark 12:30).

These three verses let us know that to be a successful Christian you must be a person who takes action.

With your might … Be firm in maintaining your ability to produce. Sounds like God doesn't think much of leisurely retirement, does He?

Work heartily … Have you ever faced a task and said, "I just don't think I have the 'heart' to do it?" When we do anything for God's work, we are to channel all our hearts, that is, *all* our willingness and ability into the task. God will provide what we cannot.

With all your mind … The great baseball philosopher Yogi Berra has been quoted as saying, "Baseball is 90 percent physical, and the other half is mental." I submit to you that success as a Christian is 100 percent mental, for our battles start in the mind. Most often the biggest obstacles to our success are manufactured in our own minds. Or more accurately, Satan places those obstacles there. Our mind is the battleground where spiritual warfare originates. Remember Isaiah 26:3: "You keep him in perfect peace, whose mind is *stayed* on you, because he trusts in you" (emphasis added).

With all your strength … If any verse suggests action, it is this one. When we think of strength, we usually think of physical ability. We may also think of mental and moral strength. All these become stronger through regular exercise. However, if we stop using our muscles (or our mental or moral capacity), they will atrophy, wither, and eventually die. While this verse may imply spiritual strength, I believe it also suggests just good old hard work.

Remember—*action* destroys fear. Let's be Christians of *action*.

God Responds

Have you ever noticed just how little you have to do for God to respond? There is a marvelous example in Psalm 18:6–20. The passage starts out, "In my distress I called upon the Lord; to my God I cried for help." David called. He did one thing. Then just look at all the things God did in response. I'll leave it to you to discover for yourself.

"For truly, I say to you, if you have faith like a grain of mustard seed, you will say to this mountain, 'Move from here to there,' and it will move, and nothing will be impossible for you" (Matt. 17:20).

When I was growing up, my dad always planted a garden in the spring, and then we worked it all summer. In the fall came the harvest. We always had fresh green beans, corn, okra, squash, cucumbers, tomatoes (you're getting hungry, right?), butter beans, and sometimes sweet peppers and cantaloupes. My dad was a world-class gardener; it seemed he could grow stuff on concrete.

It's funny; the seeds he planted were always smaller than the finished product. In relation to the size of its seed, the mustard plant grows to enormous size. Jesus is telling us that if we have this small amount of faith that we can do wonders, right? *Wrong!* He is telling us that if we have a small amount of faith and *do* something with it—in other words, couple our *action* with God's *ability* to do the impossible—*then* we can do wonders. Or more accurately, then we put ourselves in a position so that God can do wonders through us. Remember—God does not respond to our needs; those He will provide. God responds to our faith when we put it into action.

One of my favorite stories of how God responds to faith is in 2 Kings 7:3–8 (emphasis added):

> Now there were four men who were lepers at the entrance to the gate. And they said to one another [Notice, they were in agreement], "Why are we sitting here until we die? If we say, 'Let us enter the city,' the famine is in the city and we shall die there. And if we sit here, we die also. [Why are we letting fear paralyze us?] So now come, let us go over to the camp of the Syrians. If they spare our lives we shall live, and if they kill us we shall but die." [Better to die trying than to die doing nothing.] So they arose at twilight to go to the camp of the Syrians.

But when they came to the edge of the camp of the Syrians, behold, there was no one there. For the Lord had made the army of the Syrians hear the sounds of chariots and of horses, the sound of a great army, so that they said to one another, "Behold, the king of Israel has hired against us the kings of the Hittites and the kings of Egypt to come against us."

So they fled away in the twilight and abandoned their tents, their horses, and their donkeys, leaving the camp as it was, and fled for their lives. And when these lepers came to the edge of the camp, they went into a tent and ate and drank, and they carried off silver and gold and clothing and went and hid them. Then they came back and entered another tent and carried off things from it and went and hid them.

God used what these four men had—their willingness to do *something*. He took these four lepers, these four weak men who were about to die, these four men who had a legitimate excuse for not walking into the enemy's camp, and miraculously amplified the sound of their "boots on the ground," their feeble effort, and made the Syrians hear the sound of an approaching mighty army. The Syrians ran for their lives in fear, and this leprous quartet walked right into the camp and went into tent after tent after tent and found food, drink, silver, gold, fine clothing … but no Syrians!

We sometimes sing the song that says, "Well, I went to the enemy's camp and I took back what he stole from me ..." Satan has stolen from us. He has stolen our courage and given us fear instead. He has stolen our joy and given us despair. He has stolen our peace and given us turmoil. He has stolen our strength and given us weakness. He has stolen our health and given us disease. He has stolen our plenty and given us want. He has stolen our wealth and given us poverty.

Isn't it time for us to get up, march into our enemy's camp, let God amplify our action into the sound of a mighty army in lockstep with our brothers and sisters in Christ, and *take back what is ours?*

Let's put Satan on notice that he cannot paralyze us with fear any longer.

Let's put our faith into action. Now!

> One of the highest of human duties is the duty of encouragement ... It is easy to laugh at men's ideals; it is easy to pour cold water on their enthusiasm; it is easy to discourage others. The world is full of discouragers. We have a Christian duty to encourage one another. Many a time a word of praise or thanks or appreciation or cheer has kept a man on his feet. Blessed is the man who speaks such a word.[16]

CHAPTER 8

DISCUSS YOUR PROGRESS

Inevitably, once you start your quest for Christian success, the enemy will step up his own plan to attack you and try to knock you off course. This is not being negative or an admission of defeat. No! This is merely a statement of fact, and if you recognize the truth contained in it, you will be better equipped to handle Satan's attacks. You will be one step ahead of him, and often one step is all you need. So just know that you will be challenged, but also know that it is in overcoming the challenges that you will ultimately succeed.

Why *discuss* your progress? Why not *check* your progress, or *measure* your progress, or *review* your progress? Well, first it fits the clever pattern of all the other keys, but it also carries the message that we cannot succeed alone. We need the support and encouragement of our brothers and sisters in Christ. We need a support team, as we will see later. We need the special talents and abilities that other people bring to augment our own, and to support our weaknesses. We need others to help where and when we can't help ourselves. What's more, those same people need *you* and what you can bring to the table. It's *team*work: together everyone achieves more. Let's explore some of the benefits of having a good support team.

Wise Counsel

"Where there is no guidance, a people falls, but in an abundance of counselors there is safety" (Prov. 11:14).

It would serve us all well to find someone who is a successful Christian and seek his or her wise counsel. To strike out on your journey on your own without giving thought to or seeking wise advice is to invite trouble later on. "The way of a fool is right in his own eyes, but a wise man listens to advice" (Prov. 12:15).

"Without counsel purposes are disappointed: but in the multitude of counselors they are established" (Prov. 15:22 KJV). *Disappointed* here means to be frustrated, or to come to naught. How many times have you seen someone start out full of raw zeal and enthusiasm but with no real guidance and in a short while you wonder what ever happened to that person? It is better to take a little extra time to plan, train, and seek counsel. These activities will greatly increase your chances for success.

We have all seen young Christians, especially young ministers, start out like they were going to single-handedly save the world. Many times, within a few short years they have either backslidden, thought better of their calling, or were simply gone.

Established, on the other hand, means to be accomplished, finished, and complete. How much better it is when we take time to seek—and heed—wise counsel.

There is always someone available who has gone down the path on which we are about to start. They can point out the potholes and pitfalls that we cannot often see for ourselves. By seeking counsel from others, we can rely on their wisdom and experience to help us see the obstacles, and hopefully avoid them.

One quick note about seeking counsel is important here. Be very sure you are receiving counsel from those who have actually been successful in the area or areas in which you need counsel. In other words, you would not want to take financial advice from your broke brother-in-law.

Mistakes Can Be Overcome

Understand this: mistakes will happen. We cannot avoid making mistakes. The thing is, when we do make a mistake, it's not the end of the world. Everyone makes mistakes. Adam made mistakes. Moses made mistakes. David made mistakes. Peter, Paul, Silas, Barnabas, and Timothy made mistakes. Your best friend has made mistakes. (Not in choosing you as a friend, of course!) The message is not that we can avoid mistakes but that when we do make a mistake, we have resources for restoration.

"Brothers, if anyone is caught in any transgression, you who are spiritual should restore him in a spirit of gentleness. Keep watch on yourself, lest you too be tempted" (Gal. 6:1).

The *caught* in this verse is different from the woman *caught* in the act of adultery in John, chapter 8. In John, *caught* is more of an idea of being ensnared, or trapped, by a sinful act. It also carries the idea of the scribes and Pharisees who did the "catching" assuming ownership of the woman's sin, as if that gave them the right to bring it to Christ. (I have always wondered why they did not also bring the man to Jesus, but that's another topic for another day.) Sin will take you further than you planned to go, hold you longer than you planned to stay, and cost you more than you planned to pay.

In Galatians, however, *caught* has the thought of prevention, as in seeing a brother or sister headed for sin and gently and lovingly warning them of the dangers of continuing on their path. Wiser, compassionate brothers and sisters, who may have experienced the same or similar sin, should be able to encourage and restore the one who is caught in sin's web before they are permanently ensnared. Beware of the caution, however, to "keep watch on yourself," because it is easy to condemn and condescend the one we should be trying to restore. Restore in love and humility, for as Paul states, we may need restoring at some point in the future ourselves. No one likes correction, but it is often necessary and always beneficial.

Share the Load

Building on the idea that we are all members of one body, when one of us hurts, we all should feel that same hurt and do what it takes to help that hurting member heal.

"Bear one another's burdens, and so fulfill the law of Christ" (Gal. 6:2).

I cannot do your work. I cannot fulfill your purpose. That is yours alone. Neither can you do my work. But we can all help share each other's burdens, or literally each other's "load."

Did you know that two people lifting an object together can lift more total weight than they can lift separately? This phenomenon is known as *synergy,* and it says that if you can lift one hundred pounds and I can lift one hundred pounds, together we can lift not just two hundred but perhaps two hundred and fifty or even three hundred pounds. When people work together, their strengths and talents are not simply added but multiplied.

On a spiritual plane, talents and strengths are not simply added or multiplied, but increased exponentially. "You shall chase your enemies, and they shall fall before you by the sword. Five of you shall chase a hundred, and a hundred of you shall chase ten thousand, and your enemies shall fall before you by the sword …" (Lev. 26:7–8).

Now, a hundred is twenty times more than five, so if five can chase a hundred, then logically a hundred should be able to chase two thousand, right? *Wrong!* God does not operate according to our logic. He promises that when we team up with our brothers and sisters in the right spirit, He will step in and increase our efforts supernaturally. Remember the four lepers marching into the Syrians' camp?

In bearing one another's burdens we all must be willing to open up and be honest with each other. James tells us to confess our faults (sins) to one another … so you can have something to talk about? So you can say, "I knew they wouldn't make it"? So you can say, "Did you hear about …"?

No no no!

The verse continues, "… and pray for one another, that you may be healed."

Now healed in this sense can be either physically or spiritually. The point is that in confessing a fault, once the fault is exposed it can then be eliminated, but only if we do what we are supposed to do, as the Scripture commands.

So, instead of having something to talk about, we have something to pray about. Instead of saying, "I knew they wouldn't make it," we can say, "God, help them to make it." Instead of saying, "Did you hear about so and so?" we can say, "Let's pray for them."

The Mastermind Principle

In his book *The Master Key to Riches*, Napoleon Hill talks about what he calls the "Mastermind Principle." He describes it like this: when you set out to accomplish a goal, you should find a group of like-minded people—people who can help you reach your goal—and meet with them regularly to assess how you are doing and make corrections and adjustments as necessary.

To be successful as Christians, we can't do it alone. We must have help. I believe God designed us that way. As we have already seen, when we work with others, we can do much more than we could ever do by ourselves.

So what should our own "mastermind group" look like? First, we need someone to agree with us. Now, I am not talking about having a "yes person," someone who only tells us what they think we want to hear. Consider Matthew 18:19–20: "Again I say to you, if two of you agree on earth about anything they ask, it will be done for them by my Father in heaven. For where two or three are gathered in my name, there am I among them."

Let's focus on the word *agree* for just a moment. The Greek word translated to agree is *sumphoneo,* from which we get *symphony*. It implies a harmonious agreement, like instruments in a band. If an orchestra consisted of just one family of instruments, for example, all trumpets, we would not get the full effect of the music. Likewise, if all the instruments in the orchestra played exactly the same note, there would not be the beautiful blending and the rich symphony we normally expect. It takes all the instruments, each contributing their own particular part of the music, and all in perfect, harmonious agreement.

On the other hand, if even one musician went rogue and tried to play whatever notes popped into his or her head, it would soon sound like the Mayberry Band gearing up for an impromptu Sunday afternoon concert.

But when everything agrees, a beautiful symphony emerges. In a well-trained choir—with the basses laying the foundation, the tenors adding brightness, the altos bringing richness, and the sopranos providing those angelic high notes—*that* level of agreement produces a wonderful sound.

So it is when we have our mastermind group to "agree" with us. Again, these are not "yes people." Often they may tell us things that we do not want to hear, but they may be the very words we need to hear to keep us on track, or to keep us from making a huge mistake. We need someone to augment our own prayers, someone to fill in where we are weak. We must learn to rely on the particular strengths, talents, and wisdom of others.

"And he gave the apostles, the prophets, the evangelists, the shepherds and teachers, to equip the saints for the work of ministry, for building up the body of Christ" (Eph. 4:11–12).

Each of these gifts was placed in the church for a particular purpose. Since we are all familiar with pastors and teachers, let's focus on these for just a moment. Our pastor is not there just to preach to us on Sunday morning. Our teacher is not there just to fill up an hour or so on Sunday morning. There is an awesome responsibility that accompanies the work of a pastor or teacher. When a pastor or teacher stands before a congregation or a class, that person must know that he or she has sought God for His will for the message or lesson. He or she must have studied the Word for the truth it contains, prayed for the anointing to preach or teach, and prayed for the congregation or class. We need to hear what our pastors or teachers have to say because they are saying what God has given them to pass along to us. This will help us all become successful.

Just as our pastors and teachers must prepare, they must also be an example. We will not go where we are not led. As the apostle Paul said, "Brothers, join in imitating me, and keep your eyes on those who walk according to the example you have in us" (Phil. 3:17).

Paul was not being arrogant or vain in saying this. He was saying as long as he is following Christ and His example, those who follow can feel safe following him (Paul), or anyone else doing likewise. We should never follow anyone who is not closely following Jesus Christ; neither should they be part of our mastermind group.

Encourage One Another

We all know what a positive effect an encouraging word can have on us. When someone says, "You can do it!" or

"I believe in you!" it helps us find renewed strength and determination to carry on. We really begin to believe we can do it when we continually hear that kind of encouragement.

"And let us consider how to stir up one another to love and good works, not neglecting to meet together, as is the habit of some, but encouraging one another, and all the more as you see the Day drawing near" (Heb. 1:24–25).

I once heard a story about geese and why they fly in a *V* formation. They do so because it enables them to fly more efficiently than they could when flying alone, in a straight line, or just randomly. Studies show that geese can fly up to 71 percent farther whey they fly in a *V.*

At times, a flock of geese will fly over our house, and we can hear them honking at each other. What they are actually doing is honking out encouragement to the goose on the point of the *V,* the lead goose. I can just imagine them saying, "*Honk, honk,* you can do it!" and "*Honk, honk*, just a little bit farther!" and "*Honk, honk*, you're doing great!"

Notice too that the *V* formation only works when the geese fly together as a team. It won't work if just one goose stays on the ground and says, "Well, I just don't feel like flying today" or, "Well, I just don't know if I can fly alongside Brother John Goose or Sister Mary Goose."

Just like geese, we can "fly" much farther, faster, and with less effort if we depend upon others, and allow others to depend upon us.

"Anxiety in a man's heart weighs him down, but a good word makes him glad, one who is righteous is a guide to his neighbor, but the way of the wicked leads them astray" (Prov. 12:25–26).

A weighed-down heart—depression—can grip even the strongest Christian from time to time. Just being a Christian does not exempt us from trouble or the attacks of Satan; in fact, the stronger in Christ one becomes, the stronger Satan's attacks will become. But there is an antidote—a good word of encouragement. For example, if you know someone going through a tough health battle, you might tell him or her something like, "I know this is tough for you right now, but I want you to know I am praying for you and I would love to help you in any way I can."

We have already seen that we should encourage one another, but what does that involve? It may be as simple as patting someone on the back and telling that person how much you appreciate him or her, or that he or she is a blessing to your life, or just telling the person that he or she looks nice. Now, doesn't the simple act of complimenting someone make you feel good? We all like to be told how great we are, so why do we hesitate to tell someone else? We will reap what we sow. If we sow discord, we reap discord. If we sow depression, we reap depression. *When we sow encouragement, we reap encouragement.*

The word *glad* in Proverbs 12:25 literally means to "brighten up." I love to get up on a Saturday morning and open all the blinds and let the sunshine stream in. That is just how an encouraging word can affect someone; it can make a person's whole "house" feel brighter and more cheerful. And when we're happy, it's easier to pass that happiness along.

So let's remember as we discuss our progress:

- We're going to have challenges on our journey toward Christian success.
- We're going to make mistakes, but they do not have to be fatal.
- We need a mastermind group, a support team, to help us.
- We need to encourage one another along our way.
- We should be ready and willing to help share one another's burdens.

If we will do these things, we will be well on our way to achieving success as Christians, and to helping someone else achieve success as well.

In the Christian life, it's not how you start that matters. It's how you finish.

John Bisagno has been pastoring First Baptist of Houston for a number of years. When John was just about to finish college, he was having dinner over at his fiancé's house one night. After supper, he was talking with his future father-in-law, Dr. Paul Beck, out on the porch. Dr. Beck had been in the ministry for years, and that was inevitably the subject toward which the conversation turned.

"John, as you get ready to enter the ministry, I want to give you some advice," Dr. Beck told the younger man. "Stay true to Jesus! Make sure that you keep your heart close to Jesus every day. It's a long way from here to where you're going to go, and Satan's in no hurry to get you ... It has been my observation that just one out of ten who start out in full-time service for the Lord at twenty-one are still on track by the age of sixty-five."

In the Christian life, it's not how you start that matters. It's how you finish.

You may be thinking, "... I'm not in full-time ministry." I'm sorry to rock your boat, but if you are a Christian, and if you are serious about following Christ, then you surely are in the ministry. Full-time … *the enemy just doesn't want you to realize it.*

You may not collect your paycheck from a church each week, but according to Ephesians 4:11–13 and Colossians 3:23, that's not the issue. Whatever your profession, if you know Jesus Christ as your Lord and Savior, then you ultimately work for Him.

Jesus said that *you* are the light of the world. Jesus said that *you* are the salt of the earth. And He didn't mention anything about "part-time."

Now here's my question to you, and I want you to think about it carefully.

What makes you think that you will be the one out of ten who finishes strong?

What makes you think that you won't be one of the nine who fall short of the mark? The man who finishes strong, after all, is the exception. Why? Because *when it comes to finishing strong, the odds are against you.* Finishing strong is not impossible. It is, however, improbable. It's going to take some tough choices and an experience or two of personal brokenness in order to have a strong finishing kick when you hit the tape at age sixty-five, seventy-five, eighty-five, or whenever it is that God calls you home.

- It is the rare man who finishes strong.
- It is the exceptional man who finishes strong.
- It is the teachable man who finishes strong.

So here's the question. What *exceptional measures* are you taking in your life to ensure that you will be the one out of ten?[17]

The Time Factor

Any athlete knows the last minutes of a contest are the most crucial. How many games have been decided after the two-minute warning? As the game approaches a conclusion, strength is often spent. It would be easy for the athlete to yield, to give up, and throw in the towel. But if he's looking to win, he hangs tough to the end. This is the time for his best shot.

Our culture emphasizes retirement, encouraging us to hang up the spikes and enjoy a fantasy fling. Even this is contrary to the game plan. In most cases when the two-minute warning sounds, the contest intensifies. For some, this is true of life as well. Ninety-four year old Simon of Cambridge illustrates this view as he said, "I cannot but run with all my might for I am close to the goal."[18]

Never confuse activity with accomplishment. In the game of life, as in the game of football, it's results that count."

—Gene Stallings,
former head football coach,
University of Alabama

CHAPTER 9

DELIVER YOUR PROOF

I hesitate to say that we have reached the end of our journey because this is a journey that should never end. When this life has ended, we will just have begun our new, eternal lives where we will live forever and ever with our Lord and Savior, Jesus Christ. Even in this present life, we should never feel that we have "arrived." We should never assume that we have learned it all. We should never feel that we have, at last, succeeded. By now you should realize that success is not a destination you reach but a journey you take. It is a lifelong process, for the more we learn about Jesus Christ and what it takes to be successful as Christians, the more we realize that there is still so much more to learn and *do*.

I hope by now you have *discovered your purpose, declared your principles, determined your priorities, described your prize, decided your price, developed your plan,* and *deployed your parachute* and that you are regularly *discussing your progress.* Let me urge you to go back from time to time and revisit each of these keys to successful Christian living. Rediscover and reaffirm your purpose, and make sure you are doing everything you must to fulfill that purpose. Remember that it is only in doing what God has called you to do that you can hope to achieve true success as a Christian.

So what does all this mean? We have the keys. We have the knowledge. We have God's Word. What does that mean to you? What are you supposed to do with all this knowledge and all these keys? Well, I have an answer for you that you may or may not like: *that's up to you!*

I don't mean to be sarcastic or simplistic, but it really is up to you to decide what you will do with all this information. God has called you to a purpose. Now don't get hung up on the word *called*. I'm not saying you should or will have a pulpit ministry or a paid staff position. What I *am* saying is that each one of us has a work to do for God, a specific *something* that no one else can do just like you. So it really is up to *you* as an individual to decide whether or not you will find that *something*, and ultimately *deliver your proof.*

So what does this mean? In setting and achieving a goal, your proof is having reached the goal. In living successfully as a Christian, it is simply living up to the standards God sets out for us in His Word. We will now explore a few of those standards.

Endure to the End

In the previous chapter, I mentioned that a lot of people start out full of zeal and enthusiasm, only to come face-to-face with reality after a short period of time, and not being equipped to handle difficulty, they give up and lose out. The writer of Hebrews warns us against just such an eventuality.

"For we have come to share in Christ, *if indeed we hold our original confidence firm to the end*" (Heb. 3:14; emphasis added).

Since our confidence is based in God our Father, on Jesus Christ the Solid Rock, and the perfect leading and guidance of the Holy Spirit, there is no reason we should ever lose our confidence. Do you remember when you were saved? What a wonderful, almost indescribable joy! We should have the same joy and assurance of salvation now as we did the very day we were saved. In fact, our confidence should be greater now than it was then, for we have seen what God will do for us to ensure our success.

"Let us hold fast the confession of our hope without wavering, for he who promised is faithful" (Heb. 10:23).

At that time in the history of the Christian Church, there were many who had given up the fight. Religious persecution was rampant, to the point that people were being killed for their testimony as Christians. The writer is encouraging readers not to give up, not to grow weary and revert to Judaism and resume living under the curse of the law. He reminds them that Christ is faithful to fulfill His promises. Knowing Christ's faithfulness, we should be faithful to our calling. Wavering could mean anything from merely adopting a "low profile" so as not to draw attention to ourselves as Christians to total renunciation of the grace of Christ.

Many Christians around the world today are facing severe persecution, sometimes death, as a result of their testimony. In America, we may never have to face such persecution. But what if we do? Will we be firm in our confidence? Will we be successful as Christians?

Bear Fruit

What then is the visible, tangible evidence of not having given up? What can we offer as proof that we are keeping the faith? What are the outward signs of our success as Christians? Jesus often spoke of the successful disciple as one who "bears fruit."

At the time Jesus lived on earth, the Middle East was largely an agrarian society, meaning that agriculture played a vital role in the people's way of life. Vegetables, grains, and fruit of all kinds were grown and harvested for consumption and trade. It is not unusual that Jesus would use fruit trees as the subjects of some of His parables and lessons.

In order for a tree to bear fruit, certain conditions must exist. First, the branch on which the fruit grows must be attached and connected to a firm, healthy root system; that is, it must be part of a healthy tree or vine. Often, especially in vineyards, skilled and experienced vinedressers would graft branches onto proven rootstock so the new branches could begin producing fruit in a shorter period of time than if they were planted individually and left to grow and mature on their own. The host rootstock was already healthy and established.

A branch that did not produce fruit would be cut off from the main vine and used for firewood or kindling. It was not the fault of the vine if the branch did not produce fruit, for that was not the purpose of the vine. It was, however, the purpose of the branch to receive its life from the vine and in turn produce bountiful fruit.

"I am the true vine, and my Father is the vinedresser. Every branch in me that does not bear fruit he takes away, and every branch that does bear fruit he prunes, that it may bear more fruit" (John 15:1–2).

"Search me, O God, and know my heart! Try me and know my thoughts! And see if there be any grievous way in me, and lead me in the way everlasting" (Ps. 139:23).

The purpose of pruning was to remove any nonproductive or dead branches from the vine. Branches such as these would continue to draw nutrients from the vine, and in doing so, rob the other, still productive branches.

The process of pruning or removing those dead, nonproductive parts of our lives is vital if we are to continue to bear good fruit. Life today is complicated, with family, career, education, leisure activities, church, community, and a whole host of activities vying for our time. All these seem important, and they are, but sometimes we get so busy that we forget that our relationship with God must come first. We must continually seek God and ask Him to search us, know our hearts, and take away anything that is sapping the life from us.

"By this my Father is glorified, that you bear much fruit and so prove to be my disciples" (John 15:8).

The purpose for our bearing fruit is not for personal gain or glory, or for show. The sole purpose in bearing fruit is to glorify God. In fact, everything we do should be to bring glory to God the Father. That is our purpose for existing. What could be more glorious than to fulfill the purpose for which God called us—to bring forth good fruit that glorifies our Father?

"You did not choose me, but I chose you and appointed you that you should go and bear fruit and that your fruit should abide, so that whatever you ask the Father in my name, he may give it to you" (John 15:16).

There is no greater proof that we can deliver than constantly bearing fruit and seeing our fruit abide. The world should be able to see Christ's nature reproduced in our lives. Which leads to the question, *what do we look like as fruitful, successful Christians?* What are the attributes and characteristics of a successful Christian? Are there identifiable traits? The answer, of course, is a resounding *yes!*

The Nature of the Fruit

As a successful, fruitful Christian—one who is filled with and controlled by the Holy Spirit—you will manifest good fruit in three areas:

1. Your relationship with God
2. Your relationship with other people (your neighbors)
3. Your personal life

Let's examine each of these areas in some detail.

"But the fruit of the Spirit is love, joy, peace, patience, kindness, goodness, faithfulness, gentleness and self-control; against such things there is no law" (Gal. 5:22–23).

Now, the *but* that starts verse 22 refers to verse 19, which starts, "Now the works of the flesh are evident," or as we could say, "obvious" or "apparent." Should not we, as successful Christians, be just as obvious, apparent, and evident in allowing the Holy Spirit to work in our lives? Of course we should, and it all starts with a right relationship with God the Father. The Greek words from which each of these fruits is translated are shown in parentheses in the following passages.

The Fruit of Godly Relationship

Love (*agape*: God is love)—This is the kind of love that is only possible when we allow God to love through us. The passage, 1 John 4:7, tells us to *love one another* because God is love. Jesus told His disciples that we would be known by our love for one another. Can we truly love apart from God?

Joy (*chara*: cheerfulness, delight)—The word *joy* implies a calm delight; in other words, it means a deep, settled assurance that one's soul and spirit are in agreement and harmony with the Holy Spirit.

Joy is not the same as happiness. Happiness depends on how we choose to respond to circumstances, or what "happens" to us. Joy, on the other hand, is not dependent upon outside circumstances but upon our faith in Jesus Christ. The *joy* of the Lord is our strength. In His presence is fullness of *joy*. They that sow in tears shall reap in *joy*. Peter writes about *joy* unspeakable.

Certainly the successful Christian should have the calm delight—that is, the *joy*—of the Lord fully apparent in his or her life.

Peace (*eirene*: to join; by implication, security, safety, prosperity)—Only when we are joined in fellowship with God and our brothers and sisters in Christ can we know true and lasting peace. Like the bumper sticker slogan "*No Jesus, No Peace. Know Jesus, Know Peace.*"

Peace is not simply the absence of conflict, but can be defined as joy, or calm delight, in the midst of conflict.

Knowing Jesus is there to fight our battles and that He has already secured complete victory, what a peace and comfort that should be!

The Fruit of Relationship with Others

Once our relationship with God is settled and secure, we can then develop our relationship with our brothers and sisters in Christ, and our neighbor as well.

Patience (*makrothumia:* from two root words—*macros*, meaning long, as in time, and *thumos*, meaning passion, as in wrath)—The idea is that if we are long-suffering with our neighbor, our wrath will be long in coming. Remember the seven-times-seventy lesson Jesus taught Peter. This is not to say we are to let people take needless advantage of us, but if we are wronged, we should first let love, joy, and peace begin to work, and at the same time, we should pray for the one who wronged us.

Kindness (*chrestotes*: usefulness, excellence in character or demeanor)—What greater description of ourselves could we ever hope for than an excellent character? Not just a reputation, for that is just someone's opinion of who her or she thinks we are. Our reputation may not reflect our true selves. Our character reflects how we treat other people, how we do what we say we will do, and how we are truthful in all situations. These are the marks of a successful Christian. A person of excellent character, especially a Christian, will not want to harm or hurt another person; therefore, kindness will always be his or her guide.

Goodness (*agathosune*: virtue or beneficence)—Virtue, along with character and slowness to anger, are the characteristics that mark a successful Christian's relationship with his or her fellow human beings. Goodness simply tells us to be of high moral character and have a good and gentle spirit when dealing with others. But we can only demonstrate a right relationship with others by first having a right relationship with God. How we treat others ultimately reveals how strong our relationship is with God.

Once our relationship with God is secure, and we know how to treat our brothers and sisters in Christ and our non-Christian neighbors, we can learn to grow and maintain our own character through the final three fruits.

The Fruit of Our Personal Life

Faithfulness (*pistis*: conviction of the truth of anything; character of one who can be relied on)—Faithfulness (or as King James translates it, faith) starts with absolute belief in God and His Word. Without faithfulness, everything we attempt to build will eventually crumble. As we have seen, our faith must be in God Himself, not so much in what we think He can or will do for us.

A second aspect of faithfulness goes back to our character. Are we faithful in serving the Lord; that is, are we faithful with our giving, our time, and our service to others? Do we always do what we say we will do? It seems that if our *faith* in God is absolute, then our personal *faithfulness* will follow.

Gentleness (*praotes*: gentleness, humility)—We seem to have trouble with this one. Maybe it is because we also know this fruit as *meekness*, which brings to mind the image of a Walter Mitty type of person, one who lets others have free rule and reign over his life. This is, however, far from the true meaning of gentleness. Gentleness is *not* a synonym for weakness. True gentleness/meekness is more of a quiet, controlled power, one that knows when to act and when not to act. As we read in Proverbs 15:1, "A soft [gentle] answer turns away wrath, but a harsh word stirs up anger."

Self-Control (*egkrateia*: self-control, the virtue of one who masters his desires and passions)—Now here we have an apparent paradox. As Christians we are to allow the Holy Spirit to control us, letting God rule and reign in our lives. But here Paul is saying when the Spirit is fully working in the Christian, one of the traits the Christian will exhibit is self-control. How do we resolve this dilemma?

It is true, the Holy Spirit will control our lives, but only to the extent we allow Him to do so. When we become Christians, even Spirit-filled ones, we do not lose our self-will. We must subject our will to that of God's, but this is a conscious act on our part. God will not force His will on us. We must, therefore, exercise a measure of self-control in order for the Spirit of God to have full control.

Self-control also speaks of our having mastery over our sensual feelings and emotions. Just because we are saved, even Spirit-filled, does not exempt us from temptations and attacks from our enemy. When these things come against us, it is our duty to show restraint and resist the devil, first submitting to God (James 4:7).

So, the proof of the successful Christian is as follows:

1. A right relationship with God, for this is where it all begins.
2. A right relationship with our fellow humans, for this is where we demonstrate those characteristics of a successful Christian.
3. A right personal life, one that exhibits faith, a deep, settled belief in what we are doing, a controlled strength, and a self-controlled, Spirit-controlled life.

Finally, remember that we are admonished in the Word to endure to the end, hold fast to what we believe, and bear the good fruit of a successful Christian.

CHAPTER 10

PUTTING IT ALL TOGETHER

My own journey of nurturing this effort from the first seed of an idea has been long, as I sometimes struggled through several iterations—Toastmaster's International local chapter speech, Sunday school class at my church, adult Christian education class (also at my church), a presentation as a workshop to a group of American Sign Language professionals—through at least one computer crash, and finally through simply finding time to sit down long enough to bring it to fruition.

My hope and prayer for you is that you will be inspired to begin, or resume, your own journey. God has placed a dream inside your soul, of that I am convinced. Please do not die with that dream unfulfilled. Begin today. It is never too late, and you just might find renewed strength, energy, and inspiration to make your dream happen. Or, more correctly, may I say that you will find the strength, energy, and inspiration to trust God to help you fulfill your dream.

Begin today to *discover your purpose* and find that unique dream.

Build your foundation and *declare your principles*, those never-changing guideposts that will keep you true to your goals and dreams.

Then, *determine your priorities*, never forgetting to put God first in everything you do. Don't forget your family, as they are really all you have in this life.

Take some time, think carefully, and adequately *describe your prize*. If you cannot articulate your dream in clear, concise terms, you really do not understand it.

Every noble undertaking will exact from you a cost, so *decide your price* early in the process. You will either decide your dream is worth the price or it is not.

Next, thoroughly *develop your plan*, for the more time you spend here, the less you will be frustrated later on. Know where you should be at any time along the way.

Nothing happens without someone taking action, so *deploy your parachute*. Just go get it done. Plans sitting on shelves never accomplished much.

Get advice; build your mastermind group, and *discuss your progress*. Regular checkups along your journey will prove invaluable.

Finally, *deliver your proof.* Show the world your results, your success, *your dream fulfilled*.

NOTES

1   John-Roger and Peter McWilliams, *Life 101* (Los Angeles: Prelude Press, 1991), 211.

2   David Ferguson, *Kingdom Calling* (Austin, TX: Relationship Press, 2004), vii.

3   Charles F. Pfeiffer, *Old Testament History* (Grand Rapids, MI: Baker Book House, 1973), 427–432. Used by permission.

4   Stephen R. Covey, A. Roger Merrill, and Rebecca R. Merrill, *First Things First* (New York: Simon and Schuster, 1994), 75.

5   Charles Capps, *Releasing the Ability of God through Prayer* (Tulsa, OK: Harrison House, 1978), 38.

6   Dennis Waitley, *The Psychology of Winning* (New York: Berkley, 1979), 78–79.

7   Derek Williams, ed., *New Concise Bible Dictionary* (Downer's Grove, IL: Inter-Varsity Press, 1989), 128.

8   Ibid., 113.

9   Bill O'Reilly and Martin Dugard, *Killing Jesus, A History* (New York; MacMillian USA, 2013), Kindle Edition.

10   *The New Testament, an Expanded Translation*, trans. Kenneth S. Wuest (Grand Rapids, MI: Erdman, 1961).

11   Glenn Bland, *SUCCESS! The Glenn Bland Method* (Carol Stream, IL: Tyndale House, 2010), 41–42.

12   Peter J. Daniels, *How to Reach Your Life Goals* (Tulsa, OK: Honor Books, 1995), 56.

13   Og Mandino, *THE GREATEST SECRET IN THE WORLD* (Bantam Books, 1972). Used by permission of Bantam Books,

an imprint of Random House, a division of Random House LLC. All rights reserved.

14 Susan Jeffers, PhD, *Feel the Fear and Do It Anyway* (Santa Monica, CA: Jeffers Press, 1987), 13–16.

15 *The New Testament, an Expanded Translation*, trans. Kenneth S. Wuest (Grand Rapids, MI: Erdman, 1961).

16 William Barclay, *The Letter to the Hebrews, The Daily Bible Study* (Edinburgh: St. Andrews Press, 1995), 137.

17 Steve Farrar, *FINISHING STRONG: FINDING THE POWER TO GO THE DISTANCE* (WaterBrook Multnomah, 1996). Used by permission of WaterBrook Multnomah, an imprint of the Crown Publishing Group, a division of Random House LLC. All rights reserved.

18 Don Anderson, *Drawing Closer, Growing Stronger*, 1997, Multnomah, Colorado Springs, CO, 110-111.

SUGGESTIONS FOR FURTHER READING

Below are a few of my favorite books that I hope you will find as meaningful and relevant as I have over the years. Some are old, some are new, but all contain great wisdom. There are literally thousands of works in the genre of self-help and positive thinking. I would offer one piece of advice: if any work does not align itself with God's Word, leave it alone.

Happy reading.

Allen, James. *As a Man Thinketh*. New York: Grosset & Dunlap.

Andrews, Andy. *The Traveler's Gift: Seven Decisions That Determine Personal Success*. Nashville, TN: Thomas Nelson Publishing, 2005.

Batterson, Mark. *The Circle Maker: Praying Circles Around Your Biggest Dreams and Greatest Fears*. Grand Rapids. MI: Thomas Nelson Publishing, 2012.

Carnegie, Dale. *How to Win Friends and Influence People.* New York: Simon and Schuster Reissue Edition, 2009.

Coelho, Paulo. *The Alchemist.* New York: Harper, 2014.

Covey, Stephen R. *The 7 Habits of Highly Effective People.* New York: Simon and Schuster, 1990.

Heatherley, Joyce Landorf. *Balcony People.* Austin, TX: Balcony Publishing, 1984.

Maxwell, John C., and Jim Dornan. *Becoming a Person of Influence: How to Positively Impact the Lives of Others.* Nashville, TN: Thomas Nelson Publishers, 1997.

Schwartz, David. *The Magic of Thinking Big.* New York: Prentice Hall Press, 1965.

Printed in the United States
By Bookmasters